Proverbs
for
Parenting

Proverbs for Parenting

A Topical Guide for Child Raising from the Book of Proverbs

BARBARA DECKER

Lynn's Bookshelf

Library of Congress Catalog
Card Number 87-50633
ISBN 978-0-9618608-3-7

Lynn's Bookshelf
PO Box 2224 Boise ID 83701
208-331-1987

Printed in the United States of America

To my children,
Jared, Nathaniel and Hannah

CONTENTS

Part IV   Control of Mouth

Part V   Relationships

Part VI   Wrong Doings

Part VII   Godly Characteristics

Part VIII Prosperity

INTRODUCTION

One of the greatest things we can do for our children is to teach them God's Word. The words we speak help build our children's consciences, their understanding of God, and their view of life and the world about them.

Deuteronomy 6:6,7
And these words, which I command thee this day, shall be in thine heart:
And thou shalt teach them diligently unto thy children, and shalt talk of them when thou sittest in thine house, and when thou walkest by the way, and when thou liest down, and when thou risest up.

Clearly, instruction in God's Word is to be an integral part of a child's daily life, and not something that is limited to a special half hour of the day or reserved for a formal fellowship.

However, even with this awareness, I found it all too easy to allow many opportunities to pass that could have been used to embed God's Word in my children's minds. Opportunities to teach godly principles of life were being forfeited and replaced by, "Don't do that," "Stop," "Quit," "Quit whining," "Quit fighting," "Quit arguing," "Be quiet," "Be still."

I realize that terse commands may not be eliminated and that they have their place, but these were fast

1

becoming my habitual response and a main verbal means of discipline and training. So, to help me replace the oft repeated "Stop" and "Quit" and "Don't" and "No," I categorized wisdom from Proverbs, God's instruction to young people, into areas that would allow me to utilize the proverbs in raising my children.

If one of my boys dawdles in carrying out his task of taking the silverware out of the dishwasher and putting it in its proper place, I have the resource and option of teaching him a proverb about work, such as:

> Proverbs 6:6-8
> Go to the ant, thou sluggard; consider her ways, and be wise:
> Which having no guide, overseer, or ruler,
> Provideth her meat in the summer, and gathereth her food in the harvest.

And once I have instructed him with this proverb, perhaps later a simple reminder of the ant would suffice as encouragement. Or I could teach him:

> Proverbs 22:29
> Seest thou a man diligent in his business? he shall stand before kings; he shall not stand before mean men.

Proverbs 10:4; 13:4; 27:23 and 27 are other proverbs that will teach children the importance and benefits of work.

If my children begin arguing, rather than saying, "Quit it, you two," I can teach them:

Proverbs 17:14
The beginning of strife *is as* when one letteth
out water [as a break in a dam]: therefore
leave off contention, before it be meddled with
[gathers volume].

Of course in teaching this I would need to explain
that a break in a dam may be small and only allow a
trickle of water out, but that trickle wears away bits and
pieces of the dam and soon ends with a flood of water
escaping. Their arguing, the little verbal jabs and cuts
they have started, should be ended before it becomes a
full-scale yelling match and comes to blows.

If an older child finds himself envious, of what a peer
has acquired through theft or dishonesty, he needs to
understand that obedience to God holds the ultimate
profit and gain for his life, and that God will reward us
and meet our expectations as we reverence Him.

Proverbs 23:17
Let not thine heart envy sinners: but *be thou*
in the fear of the Lord all the day long.

A better football helmet, a perfect test score, and new
clothes, are things we may desire, but one's integrity
and honesty is more important than these. People who
acquire things through dishonest means are *not* to be
envied.

Proverbs 11:3
The integrity of the upright shall guide them:
but the perverseness of transgressors shall destroy them.

The proverbs are categorized into many areas where children need correction (Laziness, Lying), direction (Control of Self, Control of Mouth), growth in godly attributes (Wisdom, Faithfulness), and instruction (Reverence for God, Trust in God). The table of contents gives a complete listing of these areas.

Certainly not every eventuality you encounter as a parent appears in the indexed topics, but within each topic are principles to be applied to many situations. For example, neither neatness nor unthankfulness are topics listed, but neatness may be taught from other topics given such as stewardship or diligence. For correcting an unthankful child the topics of happiness, greed, or complaining may be used. It would be helpful to familiarize yourself with the different topics.

Proverbs For Parenting will give you ideas for teaching God's Word to your child regarding many subjects. Obedience is a vital and rewarding part of our children's lives. From the topic of obedience, you may teach your child benefits of obedience. He will learn to walk safely, avoid poverty and shame, and he will be honored and become wise (Proverbs 3:12; 13:18 and 19:20). The grouping of scriptures by topic makes it convenient to prepare a Bible lesson on a particular subject.

I originally compiled these proverbs for my use as a parent. It is by no means an exhaustive listing of topics or scriptures on child raising. I trust however it is complete enough to help you as a parent raise your child in the nurture and admonition of the Lord.

As a parent you will benefit from *Proverbs For Parenting* as much as your child will. You too will increase in your knowledge and application of God's Word.

Ephesians 4:15 (Amplified Version)
Rather, let our lives lovingly express truth in
all things–speaking truly, dealing truly, living
truly. Enfolded in love, let us grow up in every
way and in all things into him....

In order to teach your child a proverb you need to
understand it. That may require some study. In order
to use a proverb in a situation you have to have it in your
mind. That will require memorization. I found that
by picking one or two verses from the different topics
to study and memorize, I was prepared to teach my
children on the spot.

We desire to see our children grow to be strong, pro-
ductive, resourceful, godly men and women. We need to
instill in them attributes built upon and from the Word
of God. May this collection help you make the most
of the many opportunities you have to teach and correct your child using the Words of Life. And may your
children grow and wax strong in spirit, filled with wisdom and with the grace of God upon them. May men
be astonished at their understanding and believing–the
unfeigned faith that first dwelt in you.

PART ONE

Reverence for God

REVERENCE GOD

Proverbs 1:7

The fear of the Lord *is* the beginning of knowledge: *but* fools despise wisdom and instruction.

Proverbs 2:1-5

My son, if thou wilt receive my words, and hide my commandments with thee;

So that thou incline thine ear unto wisdom, *and* apply thine heart to understanding;

Yea, if thou criest after knowledge, *and* liftest up thy voice for understanding;

If thou seekest her as silver, and searchest for her as *for* hid treasures;

Then shalt thou understand the fear of the Lord, and find the knowledge of God.

Proverbs 3:7,8

Be not wise in thine own eyes: fear the Lord, and depart from evil.

It shall be health to thy navel, and marrow to thy bones.

Proverbs 8:13

The fear of the Lord *is* to hate evil: pride, and arrogancy, and the evil way, and the froward mouth, do I hate.

Proverbs 9:10,11

The fear of the Lord *is* the beginning of wisdom: and the knowledge of the holy *is* understanding.

For by me thy days shall be multiplied, and the years of thy life shall be increased.

Proverbs 10:27

The fear of the Lord prolongeth days: but the years of the wicked shall be shortened.

Proverbs 14:2

He that walketh in his uprightness feareth the Lord: but *he that is* perverse in his ways despiseth him.

Proverbs 14:26

In the fear of the Lord *is* strong confidence: and his children shall have a place of refuge.

Proverbs 14:27

The fear of the Lord *is* a fountain of life, to depart from the snares of death.

Proverbs 15:16

Better *is* little with the fear of the Lord than great treasure and trouble therewith.

Proverbs 15:33

The fear of the Lord *is* the instruction of wisdom; and before honour *is* humility.

Proverbs 16:6

By mercy and truth iniquity is purged: and by the fear of the Lord *men* depart from evil.

Proverbs 19:23

The fear of the Lord *tendeth* to life: and *he that hath it* shall abide satisfied; he shall not be visited with evil.

Proverbs 22:4

By humility *and* the fear of the Lord *are* riches, and honour, and life.

Proverbs 23:17

Let not thine heart envy sinners: but *be thou* in the fear of the Lord all the day long.

Proverbs 24:21

My son, fear thou the Lord and the king: *and* meddle not with them that are given to change.

Proverbs 28:14

Happy *is* the man that feareth alway: but he that hardeneth his heart shall fall into mischief.

Proverbs 31:30

Favour *is* deceitful, and beauty *is* vain: *but* a woman *that* feareth the Lord, she shall be praised.

STUDY GOD'S WORD

Proverbs 3:1-4

My son, forget not my law; but let thine heart keep my commandments:

For length of days, and long life, and peace, shall they add to thee.

Let not mercy and truth forsake thee: bind them about thy neck; write them upon the table of thine heart:

So shalt thou find favour and good understanding in the sight of God and man.

Proverbs 4:20-22

My son, attend to my words; incline thine ear unto my sayings.

Let them not depart from thine eyes; keep them in the midst of thine heart.

For they *are* life unto those that find them, and health to all their flesh.

Proverbs 7:2,3

Keep my commandments, and live; and my law as the apple of thine eye.

Bind them upon thy fingers, write them upon the table of thine heart.

Proverbs 8:32,33

Now therefore hearken unto me, O ye children: for blessed *are they that* keep my ways.

Hear instruction, and be wise, and refuse it not.

Proverbs 10:14

Wise *men* lay up knowledge: but the mouth of the foolish *is* near destruction.

Proverbs 10:29

The way of the Lord *is* strength to the upright: but destruction *shall be* to the workers of iniquity.

Proverbs 13:13

Whoso despiseth the word shall be destroyed: but he that feareth the commandment shall be rewarded.

Proverbs 13:14

The law of the wise *is* a fountain of life, to depart from the snares of death.

Proverbs 19:20

Hear counsel, and receive instruction, that thou mayest be wise in thy latter end.

Proverbs 19:21

There are many devices in a man's heart; nevertheless the counsel of the Lord, that shall stand.

Proverbs 22:17,18

Bow down thine ear, and hear the words of the wise, and apply thine heart unto my knowledge.

For *it is* a pleasant thing if thou keep them within thee; they shall withal be fitted in thy lips.

Proverbs 28:5

Evil men understand not judgment: but they that seek the Lord understand all *things.*

Proverbs 28:9

He that turneth away his ear from hearing the law, even his prayer *shall* be abomination.

TRUST IN GOD

Proverbs 3:5,6

Trust in the Lord with all thine heart; and lean not unto thine own understanding.

In all thy ways acknowledge him, and he shall direct thy paths.

Proverbs 11:28

He that trusteth in his riches shall fall: but the righteous shall flourish as a branch.

Proverbs 16:20

He that handleth a matter wisely shall find good: and whoso trusteth in the Lord, happy *is* he.

Proverbs 20:24

Man's goings *are* of the Lord; how can a man then understand his own way?

Proverbs 21:31

The horse *is* prepared against the day of battle: but safety *is* of the Lord.

Proverbs 22:17-19

Bow down thine ear, and hear the words of the wise, and apply thine heart unto my knowledge.

For *it is* a pleasant thing if thou keep them within thee; they shall withal be fitted in thy lips.

That thy trust may be in the Lord, I have made known to thee this day, even to thee.

Proverbs 28:25

He that is of a proud heart stirreth up strife: but he that putteth his trust in the Lord shall be made fat.

Proverbs 28:26

He that trusteth in his own heart is a fool: but whoso walketh wisely, he shall be delivered.

Proverbs 29:25

The fear of man bringeth a snare: but whoso putteth his trust in the Lord shall be safe.

Proverbs 30:5

Every word of God *is* pure: he *is* a shield unto them that put their trust in him.

PART TWO

Wisdom and Instruction

FOOLS AND FOLLY

Proverbs 1:7

The fear of the Lord *is* the beginning of knowledge: *but* fools despise wisdom and instruction.

Proverbs 1:22,23

How long, ye simple ones, will ye love simplicity? and the scorners delight in their scorning, and fools hate knowledge?

Turn you at my reproof: behold, I will pour out my spirit unto you, I will make known my words unto you.

Proverbs 1:32,33

For the turning away of the simple shall slay them, and the prosperity of fools shall destroy them.

But whoso hearkeneth unto me shall dwell safely, and shall be quiet from fear of evil.

Proverbs 3:35

The wise shall inherit glory: but shame shall be the promotion of fools.

Proverbs 8:5,6

O ye simple, understand wisdom: and, ye fools, be ye of an understanding heart.

Hear; for I will speak of excellent things; and the opening of my lips *shall be* right things.

Proverbs 10:1

The proverbs of Solomon. A wise son maketh a glad father: but a foolish son *is* the heaviness of his mother.

Proverbs 10:8

The wise in heart will receive commandments: but a prating fool shall fall.

Proverbs 10:10

He that winketh with the eye causeth sorrow: but a prating fool shall fall.

Proverbs 10:14

Wise *men* lay up knowledge: but the mouth of the foolish *is* near destruction.

Proverbs 10:18

He that hideth hatred *with* lying lips, and he that uttereth a slander, *is* a fool.

Proverbs 10:21

The lips of the righteous feed many: but fools die for
want of wisdom.

Proverbs 10:23

It is as sport to a fool to do mischief: but a man of
understanding hath wisdom.

Proverbs 11:29

He that troubleth his own house shall inherit the wind:
and the fool *shall be* servant to the wise of heart.

Proverbs 12:15

The way of a fool *is* right in his own eyes: but he that
hearkeneth unto counsel *is* wise.

Proverbs 12:16

A fool's wrath is presently known: but a prudent *man*
covereth shame.

Proverbs 12:23

A prudent man concealeth knowledge: but the heart of fools proclaimeth foolishness.

Proverbs 13:16

Every prudent *man* dealeth with knowledge: but a fool layeth open *his* folly.

Proverbs 13:19

The desire accomplished is sweet to the soul: but *it is* abomination to fools to depart from evil.

Proverbs 13:20

He that walketh with wise *men* shall be wise: but a companion of fools shall be destroyed.

Proverbs 14:1

Every wise woman buildeth her house: but the foolish plucketh it down with her hands.

Proverbs 14:3

In the mouth of the foolish *is* a rod of pride: but the lips of the wise shall preserve them.

Proverbs 14:7

Go from the presence of a foolish man, when thou perceivest not *in him* the lips of knowledge.

Proverbs 14:8

The wisdom of the prudent *is* to understand his way: but the folly of fools *is* deceit.

Proverbs 14:9

Fools make a mock at sin: but among the righteous *there is* favour.

Proverbs 14:16

A wise *man* feareth, and departeth from evil: but the fool rageth, and is confident.

Proverbs 14:18

The simple inherit folly: but the prudent are crowned with knowledge.

Proverbs 14:24

The crown of the wise *is* their riches: *but* the foolishness of fools *is* folly.

Proverbs 14:33

Wisdom resteth in the heart of him that hath understanding: but *that which is* in the midst of fools is made known.

Proverbs 15:2

The tongue of the wise useth knowledge aright: but the mouth of fools poureth out foolishness.

Proverbs 15:5

A fool despiseth his father's instruction: but he that regardeth reproof is prudent.

Proverbs 15:7

The lips of the wise disperse knowledge: but the heart of the foolish *doeth* not so.

Proverbs 15:14

The heart of him that hath understanding seeketh knowledge: but the mouth of fools feedeth on foolishness.

Proverbs 15:20

A wise son maketh a glad father: but a foolish man despiseth his mother.

Proverbs 15:21

Folly *is* joy to *him that is* destitute of wisdom: but a man of understanding walketh uprightly.

Proverbs 16:22

Understanding *is* a wellspring of life unto him that hath it: but the instruction of fools *is* folly.

Proverbs 17:7

Excellent speech becometh not a fool: much less do lying lips a prince.

Proverbs 17:10

A reproof entereth more into a wise man than an hundred stripes into a fool.

Proverbs 17:12

Let a bear robbed of her whelps meet a man, rather than a fool in his folly.

Proverbs 17:16

Wherefore *is there* a price in the hand of a fool to get wisdom, seeing *he hath* no heart *to it?*

Proverbs 17:21

He that begetteth a fool *doeth it* to his sorrow: and the father of a fool hath no joy.

Proverbs 17:24

Wisdom *is* before him that hath understanding; but the eyes of a fool *are* in the ends of the earth.

Proverbs 17:25

A foolish son *is* a grief to his father, and bitterness to her that bare him.

Proverbs 17:28

Even a fool, when he holdeth his peace, is counted wise: *and* he that shutteth his lips is *esteemed* a man of understanding.

Proverbs 18:2

A fool hath no delight in understanding, but that his heart may discover itself.

Proverbs 18:6

A fool's lips enter into contention, and his mouth calleth for strokes.

Proverbs 18:7

A fool's mouth *is* his destruction, and his lips *are* the snare of his soul.

Proverbs 19:1

Better *is* the poor that walketh in his integrity, than *he that is* perverse in his lips, and is a fool.

Proverbs 19:3

The foolishness of man perverteth his way: and his heart fretteth against the Lord.

Proverbs 19:10

Delight is not seemly for a fool; much less for a servant to have rule over princes.

Proverbs 19:13

A foolish son *is* the calamity of his father: and the contentions of a wife *are* a continual dropping.

Proverbs 19:29

Judgments are prepared for scorners, and stripes for the back of fools.

Proverbs 20:3

It is an honour for a man to cease from strife: but every fool will be meddling.

Proverbs 21:20

There is treasure to be desired and oil in the dwelling of the wise; but a foolish man spendeth it up.

Proverbs 22:15

Foolishness *is* bound in the heart of a child; *but* the rod of correction shall drive it far from him.

Proverbs 23:9

Speak not in the ears of a fool: for he will despise the wisdom of thy words.

Proverbs 24:7

Wisdom *is* too high for a fool: he openeth not his mouth in the gate.

Proverbs 26:1

As snow in summer, and as rain in harvest, so honour is not seemly for a fool.

Proverbs 26:3

A whip for the horse, a bridle for the ass, and a rod for the fool's back.

Proverbs 26:4

Answer not a fool according to his folly, lest thou also be like unto him.

Proverbs 26:5

Answer a fool according to his folly, lest he be wise in his own conceit.

Proverbs 26:6

He that sendeth a message by the hand of a fool cutteth off the feet, *and* drinketh damage.

Proverbs 26:7

The legs of the lame are not equal: so *is* a parable in the mouth of fools.

Proverbs 26:8

As he that bindeth a stone in a sling, so *is* he that giveth honour to a fool.

Proverbs 26:9

As a thorn goeth up into the hand of a drunkard, so *is* a parable in the mouth of fools.

Proverbs 26:11

As a dog returneth to his vomit, *so* a fool returneth to his folly.

Proverbs 26:12

Seest thou a man wise in his own conceit? *there is* more hope of a fool than of him.

Proverbs 27:3

A stone *is* heavy, and the sand weighty; but a fool's wrath *is* heavier than them both.

Proverbs 27:22

Though thou shouldest bray a fool in a mortar among wheat with a pestle, *yet* will not his foolishness depart from him.

Proverbs 28:26

He that trusteth in his own heart is a fool: but whoso walketh wisely, he shall be delivered.

Proverbs 29:9

If a wise man contendeth with a foolish man, whether he rage or laugh, *there is* no rest.

Proverbs 29:11

A fool uttereth all his mind: but a wise *man* keepeth it in till afterwards.

Proverbs 29:20

Seest thou a man *that is* hasty in his words? *there is* more hope of a fool than of him.

FOR BOYS

Proverbs 10:1

The proverbs of Solomon. A wise son maketh a glad father: but a foolish son *is* the heaviness of his mother.

Proverbs 11:16

A gracious woman retaineth honour: and strong *men* retain riches.

Proverbs 18:22

Whoso findeth a wife findeth a good *thing*, and obtaineth favour of the Lord.

Proverbs 19:13

A foolish son *is* the calamity of his father: and the contentions of a wife *are* a continual dropping.

Proverbs 20:29

The glory of young men *is* their strength: and the beauty of old men *is* the gray head.

Proverbs 21:9

It is better to dwell in a corner of the housetop, than with a brawling woman in a wide house.

Proverbs 21:19

It is better to dwell in the wilderness, than with a contentious and an angry woman.

Proverbs 31:3

Give not thy strength unto women, nor thy ways to that which destroyeth kings.

Proverbs 31:10,11

Who can find a virtuous woman? for her price *is* far above rubies.

The heart of her husband doth safely trust in her, so that he shall have no need of spoil.

FOR GIRLS

Proverbs 11:16

A gracious woman retaineth honour: and strong *men* retain riches.

Proverbs 11:22

As a jewel of gold in a swine's snout, *so is* a fair woman which is without discretion.

Proverbs 12:4

A virtuous woman *is* a crown to her husband: but she that maketh ashamed *is* as rottenness in his bones.

Proverbs 14:1

Every wise woman buildeth her house: but the foolish plucketh it down with her hands.

Proverbs 18:22

Whoso findeth a wife findeth a good *thing*, and obtaineth favour of the Lord.

Proverbs 19:13

A foolish son *is* the calamity of his father: and the contentions of a wife *are* a continual dropping.

Proverbs 19:14

House and riches *are* the inheritance of fathers: and a prudent wife *is* from the Lord.

Proverbs 21:9

It is better to dwell in a corner of the housetop, than with a brawling woman in a wide house.

Proverbs 21:19

It is better to dwell in the wilderness, than with a contentious and an angry woman.

Proverbs 31:10-31

Who can find a virtuous woman? for her price *is* far above rubies.

The heart of her husband doth safely trust in her, so that he shall have no need of spoil.

She will do him good and not evil all the days of her life.

She seeketh wool, and flax, and worketh willingly with her hands.

She is like the merchants' ships; she bringeth her food from afar.

She riseth also while it is yet night, and giveth meat to her household, and a portion to her maidens.

She considereth a field, and buyeth it: with the fruit of her hands she planteth a vineyard.

She girdeth her lions with strength, and strengtheneth her arms.

She perceiveth that her merchandise *is* good: her candle goeth not out by night.

She layeth her hands to the spindle, and her hands hold the distaff.

She stretcheth out her hand to the poor; yea, she reacheth forth her hands to the needy.

She is not afraid of the snow for her household: for all her household *are* clothed with scarlet.

She maketh herself coverings of tapestry; her clothing is silk and purple.

Her husband is known in the gates, when he sitteth among the elders of the land.

She maketh fine linen, and selleth *it*; and delivereth girdles unto the merchant.

Strength and honour *are* her clothing; and she shall rejoice in time to come.

She openeth her mouth with wisdom; and in her tongue *is* the law of kindness.

She looketh well to the ways of her household, and eateth not the bread of idleness.

Her children arise up, and call her blessed; her husband *also*, and he praiseth her.

Many daughters have done virtuously, but thou excellest them all.

Favour *is* deceitful, and beauty *is* vain: *but* a woman *that* feareth the Lord, she shall be praised.

Give her of the fruit of her hands; and let her own works praise her in the gates.

JUDGMENT

Proverbs 2:1,9

My son, if thou wilt receive my words, and hide my commandments with thee;

Then shalt thou understand righteousness, and judgment, and equity; *yea*, every good path.

Proverbs 2:6,8

For the Lord giveth wisdom: out of his mouth *cometh* knowledge and understanding.

He keepeth the paths of judgment, and preserveth the way of his saints.

Proverbs 13:23

Much food *is in* the tillage of the poor: but there is *that is* destroyed for want of judgment.

Proverbs 17:15

He that justifieth the wicked, and he that condemneth the just, even they both *are* abomination to the Lord.

Proverbs 17:23

A wicked *man* taketh a gift out of the bosom to pervert the ways of judgment.

Proverbs 18:5

It is not good to accept the person of the wicked, to overthrow the righteous in judgment.

Proverbs 19:28

An ungodly witness scorneth judgment: and the mouth of the wicked devoureth iniquity.

Proverbs 19:29

Judgments are prepared for scorners, and stripes for the back of fools.

Proverbs 21:3

To do justice and judgment *is* more acceptable to the Lord than sacrifice.

Proverbs 21:7

The robbery of the wicked shall destroy them; because they refuse to do judgment.

Proverbs 21:15

It is joy to the just to do judgment: but destruction *shall be* to the workers of iniquity.

Proverbs 24:23-25

These *things* also *belong* to the wise. *It is* not good to have respect of persons in judgment.

He that saith unto the wicked, Thou *art* righteous; him shall the people curse, nations shall abhor him:

But to them that rebuke *him* shall be delight, and a good blessing shall come upon them.

Proverbs 28:5

Evil men understand not judgment: but they that seek the Lord understand all *things.*

Proverbs 28:21

To have respect of persons *is* not good: for for a piece of bread *that* man will transgress.

Proverbs 29:4

The king by judgment establisheth the land: but he that receiveth gifts overthroweth it.

Proverbs 29:14

The king that faithfully judgeth the poor, his throne shall be established for ever.

Proverbs 29:26

Many seek the ruler's favour; but *every* man's judgment *cometh* from the Lord.

Proverbs 31:9

Open thy mouth, judge righteously, and plead the cause of the poor and needy.

KNOWLEDGE

Proverbs 1:4,5

To give subtilty to the simple, to the young man knowledge and discretion.

A wise *man* will hear, and will increase learning; and a man of understanding shall attain unto wise counsels.

Proverbs 1:7

The fear of the Lord *is* the beginning of knowledge: *but* fools despise wisdom and instruction.

Proverbs 1:32,33

For the turning away of the simple shall slay them, and the prosperity of fools shall destroy them.

But whoso hearkeneth unto me shall dwell safely, and shall be quiet from fear of evil.

Proverbs 2:3-5

Yea, if thou criest after knowledge, *and* liftest up thy voice for understanding;

If thou seekest her as silver, and searchest for her as *for* hid treasures;

Then shalt thou understand the fear of the Lord, and find the knowledge of God.

Proverbs 2:6

For the Lord giveth wisdom: out of his mouth *cometh* knowledge and understanding.

Proverbs 2:10-12,20

When wisdom entereth into thine heart, and knowledge is pleasant unto thy soul;

Discretion shall preserve thee, understanding shall keep thee:

To deliver thee from the way of the evil *man*, from the man that speaketh froward things;

That thou mayest walk in the way of good *men*, and keep the paths of the righteous.

Proverbs 5:1,2

My son, attend unto my wisdom, *and* bow thine ear to my understanding:

That thou mayest regard discretion, and *that* thy lips may keep knowledge.

Proverbs 8:5,6

O ye simple, understand wisdom: and, ye fools, be ye of an understanding heart.

Hear; for I will speak of excellent things; and the opening of my lips *shall be* right things.

Proverbs 8:10

Receive my instruction, and not silver; and knowledge rather than choice gold.

Proverbs 9:10

The fear of the Lord *is* the beginning of wisdom: and the knowledge of the holy *is* understanding.

Proverbs 10:14

Wise *men* lay up knowledge: but the mouth of the foolish *is* near destruction.

Proverbs 11:9

An hypocrite with *his* mouth destroyeth his neighbour: but through knowledge shall the just be delivered.

Proverbs 12:1

Whoso loveth instruction loveth knowledge: but he that hateth reproof *is* brutish.

Proverbs 13:16

Every prudent *man* dealeth with knowledge: but a fool layeth open *his* folly.

Proverbs 14:6

A scorner seeketh wisdom, and *findeth it* not: but knowledge *is* easy unto him that understandeth.

Proverbs 14:15

The simple believeth every word: but the prudent *man* looketh well to his going.

Proverbs 14:18

The simple inherit folly: but the prudent are crowned with knowledge.

Proverbs 15:2

The tongue of the wise useth knowledge aright: but the mouth of fools poureth out foolishness.

Proverbs 15:7

The lips of the wise disperse knowledge: but the heart of the foolish *doeth* not so.

Proverbs 15:14

The heart of him that hath understanding seeketh knowledge: but the mouth of fools feedeth on foolishness.

Proverbs 18:1

Through desire a man, having separated himself, seeketh *and* intermeddleth with all wisdom.

Proverbs 18:15

The heart of the prudent getteth knowledge; and the ear of the wise seeketh knowledge.

Proverbs 19:2

Also, *that* the soul *be* without knowledge, *it is* not good; and he that hasteth with *his* feet sinneth.

Proverbs 19:25

Smite a scorner, and the simple will beware: and reprove one that hath understanding, *and* he will understand knowledge.

Proverbs 20:15

There is gold, and a multitude of rubies: but the lips of knowledge *are* a precious jewel.

Proverbs 21:11

When the scorner is punished, the simple is made wise: and when the wise is instructed, he receiveth knowledge.

Proverbs 22:3; 27:12

A prudent *man* foreseeth the evil and hideth himself: but the simple pass on, and are punished.

Proverbs 22:12

The eyes of the Lord preserve knowledge, and he overthroweth the words of the transgressor.

Proverbs 22:17,18

Bow down thine ear, and hear the words of the wise, and apply thine heart unto my knowledge.

For *it is* a pleasant thing if thou keep them within thee; they shall withal be fitted in thy lips.

Proverbs 23:12

Apply thine heart unto instruction, and thine ears to the words of knowledge.

Proverbs 24:3,4

Through wisdom is an house builded; and by understanding it is established:

And by knowledge shall the chambers be filled with all precious and pleasant riches.

Proverbs 24:5

A wise man *is* strong; yea, a man of knowledge increaseth strength.

Proverbs 24:13,14

My son, eat thou honey, because *it is* good; and the honeycomb, *which is* sweet to thy taste:

So *shall* the knowledge of wisdom *be* unto thy soul: when thou hast found *it,* then there shall be a reward, and thy expectation shall not be cut off.

MARRIAGE AND SEX

Proverbs 2:10,16-19

When wisdom entereth into thine heart, and knowledge is pleasant unto thy soul;

To deliver thee from the strange woman, *even* from the stranger *which* flattereth with her words;

Which forsaketh the guide of her youth, and forgetteth the covenant of her God.

For her house inclineth unto death, and her paths unto the dead.

None that go unto her return again, neither take they hold of the paths of life.

Proverbs 5:3-21

For the lips of a strange woman drop *as* an honeycomb, and her mouth *is* smoother than oil:

But her end is bitter as wormwood, sharp as a twoedged sword.

Her feet go down to death; her steps take hold on hell.

Lest thou shouldest ponder the path of life, her ways are moveable, *that* thou canst not know *them*.

Hear me now therefore, O ye children, and depart not from the words of my mouth.

Remove thy way far from her, and come not nigh the door of her house:

Lest thou give thine honour unto others, and thy years unto the cruel:

Lest strangers be filled with thy wealth; and thy labours *be* in the house of a stranger;

And thou mourn at the last, when thy flesh and thy body are consumed,

And say, How have I hated instruction, and my heart despised reproof;

And have not obeyed the voice of my teachers, nor inclined mine ear to them that instructed me!

I was almost in all evil in the midst of the congregation and assembly.

Drink waters out of thine own cistern, and running waters out of thine own well.

Let thy fountains be dispersed abroad, *and* rivers of waters in the streets.

Let them be only thine own, and not strangers' with thee.

Let thy fountain be blessed: and rejoice with the wife of thy youth.

Let her be as the loving hind and pleasant roe; let her breasts satisfy thee at all times; and be thou ravished always with her love.

And why wilt thou, my son, be ravished with a strange woman, and embrace the bosom of a stranger?

For the ways of man *are* before the eyes of the Lord, and he pondereth all his goings.

Proverbs 6:24-35

To keep thee from the evil woman, from the flattery of the tongue of a strange woman.

Lust not after her beauty in thine heart; neither let her take thee with her eyelids.

For by means of a whorish woman *a man is brought* to a piece of bread: and the adulteress will hunt for the precious life.

Can a man take fire in his bosom, and his clothes not be burned?

Can one go upon hot coals, and his feet not be burned?

So he that goeth in to his neighbour's wife; whosoever toucheth her shall not be innocent.

Men do not despise a thief, if he steal to satisfy his soul when he is hungry;

But *if* he be found, he shall restore sevenfold; he shall give all the substance of his house.

But whoso committeth adultery with a woman lacketh understanding: he *that* doeth it destroyeth his own soul.

A wound and dishonour shall he get; and his reproach shall not be wiped away.

For jealousy *is* the rage of a man: therefore he will not spare in the day of vengeance.

He will not regard any ransom; neither will he rest content, though thou givest many gifts.

Proverbs 7:1-27

My son, keep my words, and lay up my commandments with thee.

Keep my commandments, and live; and my law as the apple of thine eye.

Bind them upon thy fingers, write them upon the table of thine heart.

Say unto wisdom, Thou *art* my sister; and call understanding *thy* kinswoman:

That they may keep thee from the strange woman, from the stranger *which* flattereth with her words.

For at the window of my house I looked through my casement,

And beheld among the simple ones, I discerned among the youths, a young man void of understanding,

Passing through the street near her corner; and he went the way to her house,

In the twilight, in the evening, in the black and dark night:

And, behold, there met him a woman *with* the attire of an harlot, and subtil of heart.

(She *is* loud and stubborn; her feet abide not in her house:

Now *is she* without, now in the streets, and lieth in wait at every corner.)

So she caught him, and kissed him, *and* with an impudent face said unto him,

I have peace offerings with me; this day have I payed my vows.

Therefore came I forth to meet thee, diligently to seek thy face, and I have found thee.

I have decked my bed with coverings of tapestry, with carved *works*, with fine linen of Egypt.

I have perfumed my bed with myrrh, aloes, and cinnamon.

Come, let us take our fill of love until the morning: let us solace ourselves with loves.

For the goodman *is* not at home, he is gone a long journey:

He hath taken a bag of money with him, *and* will come home at the day appointed.

With her much fair speech she caused him to yield, with the flattering of her lips she forced him.

He goeth after her straightway, as an ox goeth to the slaughter, or as a fool to the correction of the stocks;

Till a dart strike through his liver; as a bird hasteth to the snare, and knoweth not that it *is* for his life.

Hearken unto me now therefore, O ye children, and attend to the words of my mouth.

Let not thine heart decline to her ways, go not astray in her paths.

For she hath cast down many wounded: yea, many strong *men* have been slain by her.

Her house *is* the way to hell, going down to the chambers of death.

Proverbs 9:13-18

A foolish woman *is* clamorous: *she is* simple, and knoweth nothing.

For she sitteth at the door of her house, on a seat in the high places of the city,

To call passengers who go right on their ways:

Whoso *is* simple, let him turn in hither: and *as for* him that wanteth understanding, she saith to him,

Stolen waters are sweet, and bread *eaten* in secret is pleasant.

But he knoweth not that the dead *are* there; *and that* her guests *are* in the depths of hell.

Proverbs 12:4

A virtuous woman *is* a crown to her husband: but she that maketh ashamed *is* as rottenness in his bones.

Proverbs 14:1

Every wise woman buildeth her house: but the foolish plucketh it down with her hands.

Proverbs 17:1

Better *is* a dry morsel, and quietness therewith, than an house full of sacrifices *with* strife.

Proverbs 18:22

Whoso findeth a wife findeth a good *thing*, and obtaineth favour of the Lord.

Proverbs 19:13

A foolish son *is* the calamity of his father: and the contentions of a wife *are* a continual dropping.

Proverbs 19:14

House and riches *are* the inheritance of fathers: and a prudent wife *is* from the Lord.

Proverbs 21:9

It is better to dwell in a corner of the housetop, than with a brawling woman in a wide house.

Proverbs 22:14

The mouth of strange women *is* a deep pit; he that is abhorred of the Lord shall fall therein.

Proverbs 23:26-28

My son, give me thine heart, and let thine eyes observe my ways.

For a whore *is* a deep ditch; and a strange woman *is* a narrow pit.

She also lieth in wait as *for* a prey, and increaseth the transgressors among men.

Proverbs 29:3

Whoso loveth wisdom rejoiceth his father: but he that keepeth company with harlots spendeth *his* substance.

Proverbs 30:18,19

There be three *things which* are too wonderful for me, yea, four which I know not:

The way of an eagle in the air; the way of a serpent upon a rock; the way of a ship in the midst of the sea; and the way of a man with a maid.

Proverbs 30:20

Such *is* the way of an adulterous woman; she eateth, and wipeth her mouth, and saith, I have done no wickedness.

Proverbs 30:21,23

For three *things* the earth is disquieted, and for four *which* it cannot bear:

For an odious *woman* when she is married; and an handmaid that is heir to her mistress.

Proverbs 31:3

Give not thy strength unto women, nor thy ways to that which destroyeth kings.

Proverbs 31:10,11,28

Who can find a virtuous woman? for her price *is* far above rubies.

The heart of her husband doth safely trust in her, so that he shall have no need of spoil.

Her children arise up, and call her blessed; her husband *also*, and he praiseth her.

OBEDIENCE

Proverbs 1:5

A wise *man* will hear, and will increase learning; and a man of understanding shall attain unto wise counsels.

Proverbs 1:8,9

My son, hear the instruction of thy father, and forsake not the law of thy mother:

For they *shall be* an ornament of grace unto thy head, and chains about thy neck.

Proverbs 2:1-9

My son, if thou wilt receive my words, and hide my commandments with thee;

So that thou incline thine ear unto wisdom, *and* apply thine heart to understanding;

Yea, if thou criest after knowledge, *and* liftest up thy voice for understanding;

If thou seekest her as silver, and searchest for her as *for* hid treasures;

Then shalt thou understand the fear of the Lord, and find the knowledge of God.

For the Lord giveth wisdom: out of his mouth *cometh* knowledge and understanding.

He layeth up sound wisdom for the righteous: *he is* a buckler to them that walk uprightly.

He keepeth the paths of judgment, and preserveth the way of his saints.

Then shalt thou understand righteousness, and judgment, and equity; *yea*, every good path.

Proverbs 3:1-4

My son, forget not my law; but let thine heart keep my commandments:

For length of days, and long life, and peace, shall they add to thee.

Let not mercy and truth forsake thee: bind them about thy neck; write them upon the table of thine heart:

So shalt thou find favour and good understanding in the sight of God and man.

Proverbs 3:21-24

My son, let not them depart from thine eyes: keep sound wisdom and discretion:

So shall they be life unto thy soul, and grace to thy neck.

Then shalt thou walk in thy way safely, and thy foot shall not stumble.

When thou liest down, thou shalt not be afraid: yea, thou shalt lie down, and thy sleep shall be sweet.

Proverbs 4:1,2,4,5

Hear, ye children, the instruction of a father, and attend to know understanding.

For I give you doctrine, forsake ye not my law.

He taught me also, and said unto me, Let thine heart retain my words: keep my commandments, and live.

Get wisdom, get understanding: forget *it* not; neither decline from the words of my mouth.

Proverbs 4:10

Hear, O my son, and receive my sayings; and the years of thy life shall be many.

Proverbs 4:13

Take fast hold of instruction; let *her* not go: keep her; for she *is* thy life.

Proverbs 4:20-22

My son, attend to my words; incline thine ear unto my sayings.

Let them not depart from thine eyes; keep them in the midst of thine heart.

For they *are* life unto those that find them, and health to all their flesh.

Proverbs 5:1,2

My son, attend unto my wisdom, *and* bow thine ear to my understanding:

That thou mayest regard discretion, and *that* thy lips may keep knowledge.

Proverbs 6:20-23

My son, keep thy father's commandment, and forsake not the law of thy mother:

Bind them continually upon thine heart, *and* tie them about thy neck.

When thou goest, it shall lead thee; when thou sleepest, it shall keep thee; and *when* thou awakest, it shall talk with thee.

For the commandment *is* a lamp; and the law *is* light; and reproofs of instruction *are* the way of life.

Proverbs 7:1-3

My son, keep my words, and lay up my commandments with thee.

Keep my commandments, and live; and my law as the apple of thine eye.

Bind them upon thy fingers, write them upon the table of thine heart.

Proverbs 8:32-36

Now therefore hearken unto me, O ye children: for blessed *are they that* keep my ways.

Hear instruction, and be wise, and refuse it not.

Blessed *is* the man that heareth me, watching daily at my gates, waiting at the posts of my doors.

For whoso findeth me findeth life, and shall obtain favour of the Lord.

But he that sinneth against me wrongeth his own soul: all they that hate me love death.

Proverbs 9:9

Give *instruction* to a wise *man*, and he will be yet wiser: teach a just *man*, and he will increase in learning.

Proverbs 10:8

The wise in heart will receive commandments: but a prating fool shall fall.

Proverbs 10:17

He *is in* the way of life that keepeth instruction: but he that refuseth reproof erreth.

Proverbs 12:1

Whoso loveth instruction loveth knowledge: but he that hateth reproof *is* brutish.

Proverbs 12:15

The way of a fool *is* right in his own eyes: but he that hearkeneth unto counsel *is* wise.

Proverbs 13:1

A wise son *heareth* his father's instruction: but a scorner heareth not rebuke.

Proverbs 13:18

Poverty and shame *shall be to* him that refuseth instruction: but he that regardeth reproof shall be honoured.

Proverbs 15:5

A fool despiseth his father's instruction: but he that regardeth reproof is prudent.

Proverbs 15:32

He that refuseth instruction despiseth his own soul: but he that heareth reproof getteth understanding.

Proverbs 19:16

He that keepeth the commandment keepeth his own soul; *but* he that despiseth his ways shall die.

Proverbs 19:20

Hear counsel, and receive instruction, that thou mayest be wise in thy latter end.

Proverbs 21:11

When the scorner is punished, the simple is made wise: and when the wise is instructed, he receiveth knowledge.

Proverbs 22:17,18

Bow down thine ear, and hear the words of the wise, and apply thine heart unto my knowledge.

For *it is* a pleasant thing if thou keep them within thee; they shall withal be fitted in thy lips.

Proverbs 23:19,22

Hear thou, my son and be wise, and guide thine heart in the way.

Hearken unto thy father that begat thee, and despise not thy mother when she is old.

Proverbs 28:7

Whoso keepeth the law *is* a wise son: but he that is a companion of riotous *men* shameth his father.

Proverbs 29:18

Where *there is* no vision, the people perish: but he that keepeth the law, happy *is* he.

REPROOF AND CORRECTION

Proverbs 1:20,23

Wisdom crieth without; she uttereth her voice in the streets:

Turn you at my reproof: behold, I will pour out my spirit unto you, I will make known my words unto you.

Proverbs 1:29-33

For that they hated knowledge, and did not choose the fear of the Lord:

They would none of my counsel: they despised all my reproof.

Therefore shall they eat of the fruit of their own way, and be filled with their own devices.

For the turning away of the simple shall slay them, and the prosperity of fools shall destroy them.

But whoso hearkeneth unto me shall dwell safely, and shall be quiet from fear of evil.

Proverbs 3:11,12

My son, despise not the chastening of the Lord; neither be weary of his correction:

For whom the Lord loveth he correcteth; even as a father the son *in whom* he delighteth.

Proverbs 6:23

For the commandment *is* a lamp; and the law *is* light; and reproofs of instruction *are* the way of life.

Proverbs 9:8

Reprove not a scorner, lest he hate thee: rebuke a wise man, and he will love thee.

Proverbs 10:17

He *is in* the way of life that keepeth instruction: but he that refuseth reproof erreth.

Proverbs 12:1

Whoso loveth instruction loveth knowledge: but he that hateth reproof *is* brutish.

Proverbs 13:1

A wise son *heareth* his father's instruction: but a scorner heareth not rebuke.

Proverbs 13:13

Whoso despiseth the word shall be destroyed: but he that feareth the commandment shall be rewarded.

Proverbs 13:18

Poverty and shame *shall be to* him that refuseth instruction: but he that regardeth reproof shall be honoured.

Proverbs 13:24

He that spareth his rod hateth his son: but he that loveth him chasteneth him betimes.

Proverbs 15:5

A fool despiseth his father's instruction: but he that regardeth reproof is prudent.

Proverbs 15:10

Correction *is* grievous unto him that forsaketh the way: *and* he that hateth reproof shall die.

Proverbs 15:12

A scorner loveth not one that reproveth him: neither will he go unto the wise.

Proverbs 15:31

The ear that heareth the reproof of life abideth among the wise.

Proverbs 15:32

He that refuseth instruction despiseth his own soul: but he that heareth reproof getteth understanding.

Proverbs 17:10

A reproof entereth more into a wise man than an hundred stripes into a fool.

Proverbs 19:25

Smite a scorner, and the simple will beware: and reprove one that hath understanding, *and* he will understand knowledge.

Proverbs 22:15

Foolishness *is* bound in the heart of a child; *but* the rod of correction shall drive it far from him.

Proverbs 23:13,14

Withhold not correction from the child: for *if* thou beatest him with the rod, he shall not die.

Thou shalt beat him with the rod, and shalt deliver his soul from hell.

Proverbs 25:12

As an earring of gold, and an ornament of fine gold, *so is* a wise reprover upon an obedient ear.

Proverbs 27:5

Open rebuke *is* better than secret love.

Proverbs 28:9

He that turneth away his ear from hearing the law, even his prayer *shall be* abomination.

Proverbs 28:14

Happy *is* the man that feareth alway: but he that hardeneth his heart shall fall into mischief.

Proverbs 28:23

He that rebuketh a man afterwards shall find more favour than he that flattereth with the tongue.

Proverbs 29:1

He that being often reproved hardeneth *his* neck, shall suddenly be destroyed, and that without remedy.

Proverbs 29:15

The rod and reproof give wisdom: but a child left *to himself* bringeth his mother to shame.

Proverbs 29:17

Correct thy son, and he shall give thee rest; yea, he shall give delight unto thy soul.

Proverbs 30:5,6

Every word of God *is* pure: he *is* a shield unto them that put their trust in him.

Add thou not unto his words, lest he reprove thee, and thou be found a liar.

WISDOM AND UNDERSTANDING

Proverbs 1:5

A wise *man* will hear, and will increase learning; and a man of understanding shall attain unto wise counsels.

Proverbs 2:1-5

My son, if thou wilt receive my words, and hide my commandments with thee;

So that thou incline thine ear unto wisdom, *and* apply thine heart to understanding;

Yea, if thou criest after knowledge, *and* liftest up thy voice for understanding;

If thou seekest her as silver, and searchest for her as *for* hid treasures;

Then shalt thou understand the fear of the Lord, and find the knowledge of God.

Proverbs 2:6,7

For the Lord giveth wisdom: out of his mouth *cometh* knowledge and understanding.

He layeth up sound wisdom for the righteous: *he is* a buckler to them that walk uprightly.

Proverbs 2:10-12,20

When wisdom entereth into thine heart, and knowledge is pleasant unto thy soul;

Discretion shall preserve thee, understanding shall keep thee:

To deliver thee from the way of the evil *man*, from the man that speaketh froward things;

That thou mayest walk in the way of good *men*, and keep the paths of the righteous.

Proverbs 3:13-18

Happy *is* the man *that* findeth wisdom, and the man *that* getteth understanding.

For the merchandise of it *is* better than the merchandise of silver, and the gain thereof than fine gold.

She *is* more precious than rubies: and all the things thou canst desire are not to be compared unto her.

Length of days *is* in her right hand; *and* in her left hand riches and honour.

Her ways *are* ways of pleasantness, and all her paths *are* peace.

She *is* a tree of life to them that lay hold upon her: and happy *is every one* that retaineth her.

Proverbs 3:19,20

The Lord by wisdom hath founded the earth; by understanding hath he established the heavens.

By his knowledge the depths are broken up, and the clouds drop down the dew.

Proverbs 3:21

My son, let not them depart from thine eyes: keep sound wisdom and discretion.

Proverbs 3:35

The wise shall inherit glory: but shame shall be the promotion of fools.

Proverbs 4:5-9

Get wisdom, get understanding: forget *it* not; neither decline from the words of my mouth.

Forsake her not, and she shall preserve thee: love her, and she shall keep thee.

Wisdom *is* the principal thing; *therefore* get wisdom: and with all thy getting get understanding.

Exalt her, and she shall promote thee: she shall bring thee to honour, when thou dost embrace her.

She shall give to thine head an ornament of grace: a crown of glory shall she deliver to thee.

Proverbs 8:10-12

Receive my instruction, and not silver; and knowledge rather than choice gold.

For wisdom *is* better than rubies; and all the things that may be desired are not to be compared to it.

I wisdom dwell with prudence, and find out knowledge of witty inventions.

Proverbs 8:32-36

Now therefore hearken unto me, O ye children: for blessed *are they that* keep my ways.

Hear instruction, and be wise, and refuse it not.

Blessed *is* the man that heareth me, watching daily at my gates, waiting at the posts of my doors.

For whoso findeth me findeth life, and shall obtain favour of the Lord.

But he that sinneth against me wrongeth his own soul: all they that hate me love death.

Proverbs 9:9

Give *instruction* to a wise *man*, and he will be yet wiser: teach a just *man*, and he will increase in learning.

Proverbs 9:10

The fear of the Lord *is* the beginning of wisdom: and the knowledge of the holy *is* understanding.

Proverbs 9:12

If thou be wise, thou shalt be wise for thyself: but *if* thou scornest, thou alone shalt bear *it*.

Proverbs 10:1

The proverbs of Solomon. A wise son maketh a glad father: but a foolish son *is* the heaviness of his mother.

Proverbs 10:8

The wise in heart will receive commandments: but a prating fool shall fall.

Proverbs 10:13

In the lips of him that hath understanding wisdom is found: but a rod *is* for the back of him that is void of understanding.

Proverbs 10:14

Wise *men* lay up knowledge: but the mouth of the foolish *is* near destruction.

Proverbs 10:19

In the multitude of words there wanteth not sin: but he that refraineth his lips *is* wise.

Proverbs 10:23

It is as sport to a fool to do mischief: but a man of understanding hath wisdom.

Proverbs 12:8

A man shall be commended according to his wisdom:
but he that is of a perverse heart shall be despised.

Proverbs 12:15

The way of a fool *is* right in his own eyes: but he that
hearkeneth unto counsel *is* wise.

Proverbs 12:18

There is that speaketh like the piercings of a sword: but
the tongue of the wise *is* health.

Proverbs 13:1

A wise son *heareth* his father's instruction: but a scorner
heareth not rebuke.

Proverbs 13:14

The law of the wise *is* a fountain of life, to depart from
the snares of death.

Proverbs 13:15

Good understanding giveth favour: but the way of transgressors *is* hard.

Proverbs 14:6

A scorner seeketh wisdom, and *findeth it* not: but knowledge *is* easy unto him that understandeth.

Proverbs 14:8

The wisdom of the prudent *is* to understand his way: but the folly of fools *is* deceit.

Proverbs 14:16

A wise *man* feareth, and departeth from evil: but the fool rageth, and is confident.

Proverbs 14:29

He that is slow to wrath *is* of great understanding: but *he that is* hasty of spirit exalteth folly.

Proverbs 14:33

Wisdom resteth in the heart of him that hath understanding: but *that which is* in the midst of fools is made known.

Proverbs 14:35

The king's favour *is* toward a wise servant: but his wrath is *against* him that causeth shame.

Proverbs 15:2

The tongue of the wise useth knowledge aright: but the mouth of fools poureth out foolishness.

Proverbs 15:7

The lips of the wise disperse knowledge: but the heart of the foolish *doeth* not so.

Proverbs 15:20

A wise son maketh a glad father: but a foolish man despiseth his mother.

Proverbs 15:21

Folly *is* joy to *him that is* destitute of wisdom: but a man of understanding walketh uprightly.

Proverbs 15:24

The way of life *is* above to the wise, that he may depart from hell beneath.

Proverbs 15:31

The ear that heareth the reproof of life abideth among the wise.

Proverbs 15:33

The fear of the Lord *is* the instruction of wisdom; and before honour *is* humility.

Proverbs 16:16

How much better *is it* to get wisdom than gold! and to get understanding rather to be chosen than silver!

Proverbs 16:20

He that handleth a matter wisely shall find good: and whoso trusteth in the Lord, happy *is* he.

Proverbs 16:21

The wise in heart shall be called prudent: and the sweetness of the lips increaseth learning.

Proverbs 16:22

Understanding *is* a wellspring of life unto him that hath it: but the instruction of fools *is* folly.

Proverbs 16:23

The heart of the wise teacheth his mouth, and addeth learning to his lips.

Proverbs 17:10

A reproof entereth more into a wise man than an hundred stripes into a fool.

Proverbs 17:24

Wisdom *is* before him that hath understanding; but the eyes of a fool *are* in the ends of the earth.

Proverbs 17:27

He that hath knowledge spareth his words: *and* a man of understanding is of an excellent spirit.

Proverbs 18:1

Through desire a man, having separated himself, seeketh *and* intermeddleth with all wisdom.

Proverbs 18:4

The words of a man's mouth *are as* deep waters, *and* the wellspring of wisdom *as* a flowing brook.

Proverbs 18:15

The heart of the prudent getteth knowledge; and the ear of the wise seeketh knowledge.

Proverbs 19:8

He that getteth wisdom loveth his own soul: he that keepeth understanding shall find good.

Proverbs 19:20

Hear counsel, and receive instruction, that thou mayest be wise in thy latter end.

Proverbs 19:25

Smite a scorner, and the simple will beware: and reprove one that hath understanding, *and* he will understand knowledge.

Proverbs 20:5

Counsel in the heart of man *is like* deep water; but a man of understanding will draw it out.

Proverbs 21:11

When the scorner is punished, the simple is made wise: and when the wise is instructed, he receiveth knowledge.

Proverbs 21:20

There is treasure to be desired and oil in the dwelling of the wise; but a foolish man spendeth it up.

Proverbs 21:22

A wise *man* scaleth the city of the mighty, and casteth down the strength of the confidence thereof.

Proverbs 21:30

There is no wisdom nor understanding nor counsel against the Lord.

Proverbs 23:15,16

My son, if thine heart be wise, my heart shall rejoice, even mine.

Yea, my reins shall rejoice, when thy lips speak right things.

Proverbs 23:19

Hear thou, my son and be wise, and guide thine heart in the way.

Proverbs 23:23

Buy the truth, and sell *it* not; *also* wisdom, and instruction, and understanding.

Proverbs 24:3,4

Through wisdom is an house builded; and by understanding it is established:

And by knowledge shall the chambers be filled with all precious and pleasant riches.

Proverbs 24:5

A wise man *is* strong; yea, a man of knowledge increaseth strength.

Proverbs 24:13,14

My son, eat thou honey, because *it is* good; and the honeycomb, *which is* sweet to thy taste:

So *shall* the knowledge of wisdom *be* unto thy soul: when thou hast found *it*, then there shall be a reward, and thy expectation shall not be cut off.

Proverbs 24:23

These *things* also *belong* to the wise. *It is* not good to have respect of persons in judgment.

Proverbs 28:2

For the transgression of a land many *are* the princes thereof: but by a man of understanding *and* knowledge the state *thereof* shall be prolonged.

Proverbs 28:5

Evil men understand not judgment: but they that seek the Lord understand all *things*.

Proverbs 28:7

Whoso keepeth the law *is* a wise son: but he that is a companion of riotous *men* shameth his father.

Proverbs 28:11

The rich man *is* wise in his own conceit; but the poor that hath understanding searcheth him out.

Proverbs 28:16

The prince that wanteth understanding *is* also a great oppressor: *but* he that hateth covetousness shall prolong *his* days.

Proverbs 28:26

He that trusteth in his own heart is a fool: but whoso walketh wisely, he shall be delivered.

Proverbs 29:3

Whoso loveth wisdom rejoiceth his father: but he that keepeth company with harlots spendeth *his* substance.

Proverbs 29:8

Scornful men bring a city into a snare: but wise *men* turn away wrath.

Proverbs 29:9

If a wise man contendeth with a foolish man, whether he rage or laugh, *there is* no rest.

Proverbs 29:11

A fool uttereth all his mind: but a wise *man* keepeth it in till afterwards.

Proverbs 29:15

The rod and reproof give wisdom: but a child left *to himself* bringeth his mother to shame.

Proverbs 30:24-28

There be four *things which are* little upon the earth, but they *are* exceeding wise:

The ants *are* a people not strong, yet they prepare their meat in the summer;

The conies *are but* a feeble folk, yet make they their houses in the rocks;

The locusts have no king, yet go they forth all of them by bands;

The spider taketh hold with her hands, and is in kings' palaces.

PART THREE

Self-Control

ANGER

Proverbs 14:17

He that is soon angry dealeth foolishly: and a man of wicked devices is hated.

Proverbs 14:29

He that is slow to wrath *is* of great understanding: but *he that is* hasty of spirit exalteth folly.

Proverbs 15:1

A soft answer turneth away wrath: but grievous words stir up anger.

Proverbs 15:18

A wrathful man stirreth up strife: but *he that is* slow to anger appeaseth strife.

Proverbs 16:14

The wrath of a king *is as* messengers of death: but a wise man will pacify it.

Proverbs 16:32

He that is slow to anger *is* better than the mighty; and he that ruleth his spirit than he that taketh a city.

Proverbs 19:11

The discretion of a man deferreth his anger; and *it is* his glory to pass over a transgression.

Proverbs 19:19

A man of great wrath shall suffer punishment: for if thou deliver *him*, yet thou must do it again.

Proverbs 21:19

It is better to dwell in the wilderness, than with a contentious and an angry woman.

Proverbs 21:24

Proud *and* haughty scorner *is* his name, who dealeth in proud wrath.

Proverbs 22:24

Make no friendship with an angry man; and with a furious man thou shalt not go.

Proverbs 27:3

A stone *is* heavy, and the sand weighty; but a fool's wrath *is* heavier than them both.

Proverbs 27:4

Wrath *is* cruel, and anger *is* outrageous; but who *is* able to stand before envy?

Proverbs 29:8

Scornful men bring a city into a snare: but wise *men* turn away wrath.

Proverbs 29:22

An angry man stirreth up strife, and a furious man aboundeth in transgression.

Proverbs 30:33

Surely the churning of milk bringeth forth butter, and the wringing of the nose bringeth forth blood: so the forcing of wrath bringeth forth strife.

DILIGENCE

Proverbs 4:23

Keep thy heart with all diligence; for out of it *are* the issues of life.

Proverbs 10:4

He becometh poor that dealeth *with* a slack hand: but the hand of the diligent maketh rich.

Proverbs 11:27

He that diligently seeketh good procureth favour: but he that seeketh mischief, it shall come unto him.

Proverbs 12:24

The hand of the diligent shall bear rule: but the slothful shall be under tribute.

Proverbs 12:27

The slothful *man* roasteth not that which he took in hunting: but the substance of a diligent man *is* precious.

Proverbs 13:4

The soul of the sluggard desireth, and *hath* nothing: but the soul of the diligent shall be made fat.

Proverbs 21:5

The thoughts of the diligent *tend* only to plenteousness; but of every one *that is* hasty only to want.

Proverbs 22:29

Seest thou a man diligent in his business? he shall stand before kings; he shall not stand before mean *men*.

Proverbs 24:10

If thou faint in the day of adversity, thy strength *is* small.

Proverbs 27:23,27

Be thou diligent to know the state of thy flocks, *and* look well to thy herds.

And *thou shalt have* goats' milk enough for thy food, for the food of thy household, and *for* the maintenance for thy maidens.

DRINKING

Proverbs 20:1

Wine *is* a mocker, strong drink *is* raging: and whosoever is deceived thereby is not wise.

Proverbs 21:17

He that loveth pleasure *shall be* a poor man: he that loveth wine and oil shall not be rich.

Proverbs 23:20,21

Be not among wine-bibbers; among riotous eaters of flesh:

For the drunkard and the glutton shall come to poverty: and drowsiness shall clothe *a man* with rags.

Proverbs 23:29-35

Who hath woe? who hath sorrow? who hath contentions? who hath babbling? who hath wounds without cause? who hath redness of eyes?

They that tarry long at the wine; they that go to seek mixed wine.

Look not thou upon the wine when it is red, when it giveth his colour in the cup, *when* it moveth itself aright.

At the last it biteth like a serpent, and stingeth like an adder.

Thine eyes shall behold strange women, and thine heart shall utter perverse things.

Yea, thou shalt be as he that lieth down in the midst of the sea, or as he that lieth upon the top of a mast.

They have stricken me, *shalt thou say, and* I was not sick; they have beaten me, *and* I felt *it* not: when shall I awake? I will seek it yet again.

Proverbs 31:4-7

It is not for kings, O Lemuel, *it is* not for kings to drink wine; nor for princes strong drink:

Lest they drink, and forget the law, and pervert the judgment of any of the afflicted.

Give strong drink unto him that is ready to perish, and wine unto those that be of heavy hearts.

Let him drink, and forget his poverty, and remember his misery no more.

ENVY AND JEALOUSY

Proverbs 6:34,35

For envy and jealousy *is* the rage of a man: therefore he will not spare in the day of vengeance.

He will not regard any ransom; neither will he rest content, though thou givest many gifts.

Proverbs 14:30

A sound heart *is* the life of the flesh: but envy the rottenness of the bones.

Proverbs 27:4

Wrath *is* cruel, and anger *is* outrageous; but who *is* able to stand before envy?

ENVY OF EVILDOERS

Proverbs 1:31-33

Therefore shall they eat of the fruit of their own way, and be filled with their own devices.

For the turning away of the simple shall slay them, and the prosperity of fools shall destroy them.

But whoso hearkeneth unto me shall dwell safely, and shall be quiet from fear of evil.

Proverbs 2:21,22

For the upright shall dwell in the land, and the perfect shall remain in it.

But the wicked shall be cut off from the earth, and the transgressors shall be rooted out of it.

Proverbs 3:31,32

Envy thou not the oppressor, and choose none of his ways.

For the froward *is* abomination to the Lord: but his secret *is* with the righteous.

Proverbs 8:13

The fear of the Lord *is* to hate evil: pride, and arrogancy, and the evil way, and the froward mouth, do I hate.

Proverbs 10:3

The Lord will not suffer the soul of the righteous to famish: but he casteth away the substance of the wicked.

Proverbs 10:25

As the whirlwind passeth, so *is* the wicked no *more:* but the righteous *is* an everlasting foundation.

Proverbs 10:27-30

The fear of the Lord prolongeth days: but the years of the wicked shall be shortened.

The hope of the righteous *shall be* gladness: but the expectation of the wicked shall perish.

The way of the Lord *is* strength to the upright: but destruction *shall be* to the workers of iniquity.

The righteous shall never be removed: but the wicked shall not inhabit the earth.

Proverbs 11:3

The integrity of the upright shall guide them: but the perverseness of transgressors shall destroy them.

Proverbs 11:5,6

The righteousness of the perfect shall direct his way: but the wicked shall fall by his own wickedness.

The righteousness of the upright shall deliver them: but transgressors shall be taken in *their own* naughtiness.

Proverbs 11:21

Though hand *join* in hand, the wicked shall not be unpunished: but the seed of the righteous shall be delivered.

Proverbs 11:31

Behold, the righteous shall be recompensed in the earth: much more the wicked and the sinner.

Proverbs 12:7

The wicked are overthrown, and *are* not: but the house of the righteous shall stand.

Proverbs 13:9

The light of the righteous rejoiceth: but the lamp of the wicked shall be put out.

Proverbs 22:12

The eyes of the Lord preserve knowledge, and he overthroweth the words of the transgressor.

Proverbs 23:6

Eat thou not the bread of *him that hath* an evil eye, neither desire thou his dainty meats.

Proverbs 23:17,18

Let not thine heart envy sinners: but *be thou* in the fear of the Lord all the day long.

For surely there is an end; and thine expectation shall not be cut off.

Proverbs 24:1,2

Be not thou envious against evil men, neither desire to be with them.

For their heart studieth destruction, and their lips talk of mischief.

Proverbs 24:19,20

Fret not thyself because of evil *men*, neither be thou envious at the wicked;

For there shall be no reward to the evil *man*; the candle of the wicked shall be put out.

FEAR

Proverbs 1:33

But whoso hearkeneth unto me shall dwell safely, and shall be quiet from fear of evil.

Proverbs 3:21,24

My son, let not them depart from thine eyes: keep sound wisdom and discretion:

When thou liest down, thou shalt not be afraid: yea, thou shalt lie down, and thy sleep shall be sweet.

Proverbs 3:25,26

Be not afraid of sudden fear, neither of the desolation of the wicked, when it cometh.

For the Lord shall be thy confidence, and shall keep thy foot from being taken.

Proverbs 10:24

The fear of the wicked, it shall come upon him: but the desire of the righteous shall be granted.

Proverbs 29:25

The fear of man bringeth a snare: but whoso putteth his trust in the Lord shall be safe.

GREED AND COVETOUSNESS

Proverbs 1:18,19

And they lay wait for their *own* blood; they lurk privily for their *own* lives.

So *are* the ways of every one that is greedy of gain; *which* taketh away the life of the owners thereof.

Proverbs 13:25

The righteous eateth to the satisfying of his soul: but the belly of the wicked shall want.

Proverbs 15:16

Better *is* little with the fear of the Lord than great treasure and trouble therewith.

Proverbs 15:27

He that is greedy of gain troubleth his own house; but he that hateth gifts shall live.

Proverbs 22:1

A *good* name *is* rather to be chosen than great riches, *and* loving favour rather than silver and gold.

Proverbs 22:4

By humility *and* the fear of the Lord *are* riches, and honour, and life.

Proverbs 25:16

Hast thou found honey? eat so much as is sufficient for thee, lest thou be filled therewith, and vomit it.

Proverbs 27:20

Hell and destruction are never full; so the eyes of man are never satisfied.

Proverbs 28:6

Better *is* the poor that walketh in his uprightness, than *he that is* perverse *in his* ways, though he *be* rich.

Proverbs 28:8

He that by usury and unjust gain increaseth his substance, he shall gather it for him that will pity the poor.

Proverbs 28:16

The prince that wanteth understanding *is* also a great oppressor: *but* he that hateth covetousness shall prolong *his* days.

HASTE

Proverbs 4:26

Ponder the path of thy feet, and let all thy ways be established.

Proverbs 14:29

He that is slow to wrath *is* of great understanding: but *he that is* hasty of spirit exalteth folly.

Proverbs 18:13

He that answereth a matter before he heareth *it*, it *is* folly and shame unto him.

Proverbs 19:2

Also, *that* the soul be without knowledge, *it is* not good; and he that hasteth with *his* feet sinneth.

Proverbs 20:21

An inheritance *may be* gotten hastily at the beginning; but the end thereof shall not be blessed.

Proverbs 21:5

The thoughts of the diligent *tend* only to plenteousness; but of every one *that is* hasty only to want.

Proverbs 25:8

Go not forth hastily to strive, lest *thou know not* what to do in the end thereof, when thy neighbour hath put thee to shame.

Proverbs 28:20

A faithful man shall abound with blessings: but he that maketh haste to be rich shall not be innocent.

Proverbs 28:22

He that hasteth to be rich *hath* an evil eye, and considereth not that poverty shall come upon him.

Proverbs 29:20

Seest thou a man *that is* hasty in his words? *there is* more hope of a fool than of him.

HATE

Proverbs 10:12
Hatred stirreth up strifes: but love covereth all sins.

Proverbs 10:18
He that hideth hatred *with* lying lips, and he that uttereth a slander, *is* a fool.

Proverbs 11:12
He that is void of wisdom despiseth his neighbour: but a man of understanding holdeth his peace.

Proverbs 14:21
He that despiseth his neighbour sinneth: but he that hath mercy on the poor, happy *is* he.

Proverbs 15:17
Better *is* a dinner of herbs where love is, than a stalled ox and hatred therewith.

Proverbs 26:24

He that hateth dissembleth with his lips, and layeth up deceit within him.

Proverbs 26:26

Whose hatred is covered by deceit, his wickedness shall be shewed before the *whole* congregation.

JUMPING TO CONCLUSIONS

Proverbs 18:13

He that answereth a matter before he heareth *it*, it *is* folly and shame unto him.

Proverbs 25:8

Go not forth hastily to strive, lest *thou know not* what to do in the end thereof, when thy neighbour hath put thee to shame.

Proverbs 29:20

Seest thou a man *that is* hasty in his words? *there is* more hope of a fool than of him.

PRIDE

Proverbs 6:16,17

These six *things* doth the Lord hate: yea, seven *are* an abomination unto him:

A proud look, a lying tongue, and hands that shed innocent blood.

Proverbs 8:13

The fear of the Lord *is* to hate evil: pride, and arrogancy, and the evil way, and the froward mouth, do I hate.

Proverbs 11:2

When pride cometh, then cometh shame: but with the lowly *is* wisdom.

Proverbs 13:10

Only by pride cometh contention: but with the well advised *is* wisdom.

Proverbs 14:3

In the mouth of the foolish *is* a rod of pride: but the lips of the wise shall preserve them.

Proverbs 15:25

The Lord will destroy the house of the proud: but he will establish the border of the widow.

Proverbs 16:5

Every one *that is* proud in heart *is* an abomination to the Lord: *though* hand *join* in hand, he shall not be unpunished.

Proverbs 16:18

Pride *goeth* before destruction, and an haughty spirit before a fall.

Proverbs 16:19

Better *it is to be* of an humble spirit with the lowly, than to divide the spoil with the proud.

Proverbs 17:19

He loveth transgression that loveth strife: *and* he that exalteth his gate seeketh destruction.

Proverbs 18:12

Before destruction the heart of man is haughty, and before honour *is* humility.

Proverbs 21:4

An high look, and a proud heart, *and* the plowing of the wicked, *is* sin.

Proverbs 21:24

Proud *and* haughty scorner *is* his name, who dealeth in proud wrath.

Proverbs 25:6,7

Put not forth thyself in the presence of the king, and stand not in the place of great *men:*

For better *it is* that it be said unto thee, Come up hither; than that thou shouldest be put lower in the presence of the prince whom thine eyes have seen.

Proverbs 25:27

It is not good to eat much honey: so *for men* to search their own glory *is not* glory.

Proverbs 26:12

Seest thou a man wise in his own conceit? *there is* more hope of a fool than of him.

Proverbs 28:25

He that is of a proud heart stirreth up strife: but he that putteth his trust in the Lord shall be made fat.

Proverbs 29:23

A man's pride shall bring him low: but honour shall uphold the humble in spirit.

Proverbs 30:32

If thou hast done foolishly in lifting up thyself, or if thou hast thought evil, *lay* thine hand upon thy mouth.

SELFISHNESS

Proverbs 3:27,28

Withhold not good from them to whom it is due, when it is in the power of thine hand to do *it*.

Say not unto thy neighbour, Go, and come again, and to morrow I will give; when thou hast it by thee.

Proverbs 13:7

There is that maketh himself rich, yet *hath* nothing: *there is* that maketh himself poor, yet *hath* great riches.

Proverbs 19:17

He that hath pity upon the poor lendeth unto the Lord; and that which he hath given will he pay him again.

Proverbs 21:25,26

The desire of the slothful killeth him; for his hands refuse to labour.

He coveteth greedily all the day long: but the righteous giveth and spareth not.

Proverbs 22:9

He that hath a bountiful eye shall be blessed; for he giveth of his bread to the poor.

Proverbs 24:11,12

If thou forbear to deliver *them that are* drawn unto death, and *those that are* ready to be slain;

If thou sayest, Behold, we knew it not; doth not he that pondereth the heart consider *it?* and he that keepeth thy soul, doth *not* he know *it?* and shall *not* he render to *every* man according to his works?

Proverbs 28:27

He that giveth unto the poor shall not lack: but he that hideth his eyes shall have many a curse.

SELF-CONTROL

Proverbs 16:32

He that is slow to anger *is* better than the mighty; and he that ruleth his spirit than he that taketh a city.

Proverbs 21:17

He that loveth pleasure *shall be* a poor man: he that loveth wine and oil shall not be rich.

Proverbs 23:1-3

When thou sittest to eat with a ruler, consider diligently what *is* before thee:

And put a knife to thy throat, if thou *be* a man given to appetite.

Be not desirous of his dainties: for they *are* deceitful meat.

Proverbs 25:16

Hast thou found honey? eat so much as is sufficient for thee, lest thou be filled therewith, and vomit it.

Proverbs 25:27

It is not good to eat much honey: *so for men* to search their own glory *is not* glory.

Proverbs 25:28

He that *hath* no rule over his own spirit *is like* a city *that is* broken down, *and* without walls.

SELF-SATISFACTION

Proverbs 12:14

A man shall be satisfied with good by the fruit of *his* mouth: and the recompense of a man's hands shall be rendered unto him.

Proverbs 13:19

The desire accomplished is sweet to the soul: but *it is* abomination to fools to depart from evil.

Proverbs 14:14

The backslider in heart shall be filled with his own ways: and a good man *shall be satisfied* from himself.

Proverbs 16:20

He that handleth a matter wisely shall find good: and whoso trusteth in the Lord, happy *is* he.

Proverbs 21:2

Every way of a man *is* right in his own eyes: but the Lord pondereth the hearts.

SLEEPING AND RISING

Proverbs 3:21,24

My son, let not them depart from thine eyes: keep sound wisdom and discretion:

When thou liest down, thou shalt not be afraid: yea, thou shalt lie down, and thy sleep shall be sweet.

Proverbs 6:9-11

How long wilt thou sleep, O sluggard? when wilt thou arise out of thy sleep?

Yet a little sleep, a little slumber, a little folding of the hands to sleep:

So shall thy poverty come as one that travelleth, and thy want as an armed man.

Proverbs 6:20,22

My son, keep thy father's commandment, and forsake not the law of thy mother:

When thou goest, it shall lead thee; when thou sleepest, it shall keep thee; and *when* thou awakest, it shall talk with thee.

Proverbs 10:5

He that gathereth in summer *is* a wise son: *but* he that sleepeth in harvest *is* a son that causeth shame.

Proverbs 19:15

Slothfulness casteth into a deep sleep; and an idle soul shall suffer hunger.

Proverbs 20:13

Love not sleep, lest thou come to poverty; open thine eyes, *and* thou shalt be satisfied with bread.

Proverbs 24:33,34

Yet a little sleep, a little slumber, a little folding of the hands to sleep:

So shall thy poverty come *as* one that travelleth; and thy want as an armed man.

Proverbs 26:14

As the door turneth upon his hinges, so *doth* the slothful upon his bed.

TEMPER

Proverbs 16:32

He that is slow to anger *is* better than the mighty; and he that ruleth his spirit than he that taketh a city.

Proverbs 19:11

The discretion of a man deferreth his anger; and *it is* his glory to pass over a transgression.

Proverbs 25:28

He that *hath* no rule over his own spirit *is like* a city *that is* broken down, *and* without walls.

TEMPTATION

Proverbs 1:10,15

My son, if sinners entice thee, consent thou not.

My son, walk not thou in the way with them; refrain thy foot from their path.

Proverbs 3:5,6

Trust in the Lord with all thine heart; and lean not unto thine own understanding.

In all thy ways acknowledge him, and he shall direct thy paths.

Proverbs 3:7,8

Be not wise in thine own eyes: fear the Lord, and depart from evil.

It shall be health to thy navel, and marrow to thy bones.

Proverbs 4:25-27

Let thine eyes look right on, and let thine eyelids look straight before thee.

Ponder the path of thy feet, and let all thy ways be established.

Turn not to the right hand nor to the left: remove thy foot from evil.

Proverbs 8:13

The fear of the Lord *is* to hate evil: pride, and arrogancy, and the evil way, and the froward mouth, do I hate.

Proverbs 10:2

Treasures of wickedness profit nothing: but righteousness delivereth from death.

Proverbs 10:9

He that walketh uprightly walketh surely: but he that perverteth his ways shall be known.

Proverbs 11:5,6

The righteousness of the perfect shall direct his way: but the wicked shall fall by his own wickedness.

The righteousness of the upright shall deliver them: but transgressors shall be taken in *their own* naughtiness.

Proverbs 11:8

The righteous is delivered out of trouble, and the wicked cometh in his stead.

Proverbs 12:3

A man shall not be established by wickedness: but the root of the righteous shall not be moved.

Proverbs 12:13

The wicked is snared by the transgression of *his* lips: but the just shall come out of trouble.

Proverbs 14:12

There is a way which seemeth right unto a man, but the end thereof *are* the ways of death.

Proverbs 14:16

A wise *man* feareth, and departeth from evil: but the fool rageth, and is confident.

Proverbs 14:22

Do they not err that devise evil? but mercy and truth *shall be* to them that devise good.

Proverbs 15:3

The eyes of the Lord *are* in every place, beholding the evil and the good.

Proverbs 15:9

The way of the wicked *is* an abomination unto the Lord: but he loveth him that followeth after righteousness.

Proverbs 16:6

By mercy and truth iniquity is purged: and by the fear of the Lord *men* depart from evil.

Proverbs 16:8

Better *is* a little with righteousness than great revenues without right.

Proverbs 16:17

The highway of the upright *is* to depart from evil: he that keepeth his way preserveth his soul.

Proverbs 16:19

Better *it is to be* of an humble spirit with the lowly, than to divide the spoil with the proud.

Proverbs 19:1

Better *is* the poor that walketh in his integrity, than *he that is* perverse in his lips, and is a fool.

Proverbs 19:21

There are many devices in a man's heart; nevertheless the counsel of the Lord, that shall stand.

Proverbs 20:17

Bread of deceit *is* sweet to a man; but afterwards his mouth shall be filled with gravel.

Proverbs 21:15

It is joy to the just to do judgment: but destruction *shall be* to the workers of iniquity.

Proverbs 28:6

Better *is* the poor that walketh in his uprightness, than *he that is* perverse *in his* ways, though he *be* rich.

Proverbs 28:26

He that trusteth in his own heart is a fool: but whoso walketh wisely, he shall be delivered.

Proverbs 29:6

In the transgression of an evil man *there is* a snare: but the righteous doth sing and rejoice.

PART FOUR

Control
of Mouth

ARGUING AND STRIFE

Proverbs 3:30

Strive not with a man without cause, if he have done thee no harm.

Proverbs 6:16,19

These six *things* doth the Lord hate: yea, seven *are* an abomination unto him:

A false witness *that* speaketh lies, and he that soweth discord among brethren.

Proverbs 10:12

Hatred stirreth up strifes: but love covereth all sins.

Proverbs 13:10

Only by pride cometh contention: but with the well advised *is* wisdom.

Proverbs 15:18

A wrathful man stirreth up strife: but *he that is* slow to anger appeaseth strife.

Proverbs 16:28

A froward man soweth strife: and a whisperer separateth chief friends.

Proverbs 17:1

Better *is* a dry morsel, and quietness therewith, than an house full of sacrifices *with* strife.

Proverbs 17:14

The beginning of strife *is as* when one letteth out water: therefore leave off contention, before it be meddled with.

Proverbs 17:19

He loveth transgression that loveth strife: *and* he that exalteth his gate seeketh destruction.

Proverbs 18:6

A fool's lips enter into contention, and his mouth calleth for strokes.

Proverbs 18:19

A brother offended *is harder to be won* than a strong city: and *their* contentions *are* like the bars of a castle.

Proverbs 20:3

It is an honour for a man to cease from strife: but every fool will be meddling.

Proverbs 22:10

Cast out the scorner, and contention shall go out; yea, strife and reproach shall cease.

Proverbs 25:8

Go not forth hastily to strive, lest *thou know not* what to do in the end thereof, when thy neighbour hath put thee to shame.

Proverbs 25:24

It is better to dwell in the corner of the housetop, than with a brawling woman and in a wide house.

Proverbs 26:17

He that passeth by, *and* meddleth with strife *belonging* not to him, *is like* one that taketh a dog by the ears.

Proverbs 26:20

Where no wood is, *there* the fire goeth out: so where *there is* no talebearer, the strife ceaseth.

Proverbs 26:21

As coals *are* to burning coals, and wood to fire; so *is* a contentious man to kindle strife.

Proverbs 27:15

A continual dropping in a very rainy day and a contentious woman are alike.

Proverbs 28:25

He that is of a proud heart stirreth up strife: but he that putteth his trust in the Lord shall be made fat.

Proverbs 29:9

If a wise man contendeth with a foolish man, whether he rage or laugh, *there is* no rest.

Proverbs 29:22

An angry man stirreth up strife, and a furious man aboundeth in transgression.

Proverbs 30:33

Surely the churning of milk bringeth forth butter, and the wringing of the nose bringeth forth blood: so the forcing of wrath bringeth forth strife.

BOASTING

Proverbs 25:14

Whoso boasteth himself of a false gift *is like* clouds and wind without rain.

Proverbs 25:27

It is not good to eat much honey: *so for men* to search their own glory *is not* glory.

Proverbs 27:1

Boast not thyself of to morrow; for thou knowest not what a day may bring forth.

Proverbs 27:2

Let another man praise thee, and not thine own mouth; a stranger, and not thine own lips.

COMPLAINING

Proverbs 15:4

A wholesome tongue *is* a tree of life: but perverseness therein *is* a breach in the spirit.

Proverbs 15:15

All the days of the afflicted *are* evil: but he that is of a merry heart *hath* a continual feast.

Proverbs 17:22

A merry heart doeth good *like* a medicine: but a broken spirit drieth the bones.

Proverbs 21:19

It is better to dwell in the wilderness, than with a contentious and an angry woman.

Proverbs 25:24

It is better to dwell in the corner of the housetop, than with a brawling woman and in a wide house.

Proverbs 27:15

A continual dropping in a very rainy day and a contentious woman are alike.

CONTROL OF MOUTH

Proverbs 4:24

Put away from thee a froward mouth, and perverse lips put far from thee.

Proverbs 6:1,2

My son, if thou be surety for thy friend, *if* thou hast stricken thy hand with a stranger,

Thou art snared with the words of thy mouth, thou art taken with the words of thy mouth.

Proverbs 8:13

The fear of the Lord *is* to hate evil: pride, and arrogancy, and the evil way, and the froward mouth, do I hate.

Proverbs 10:11

The mouth of a righteous *man is* a well of life: but violence covereth the mouth of the wicked.

Proverbs 10:14

Wise *men* lay up knowledge: but the mouth of the foolish *is* near destruction.

Proverbs 10:19

In the multitude of words there wanteth not sin: but he that refraineth his lips *is* wise.

Proverbs 10:20,21

The tongue of the just *is as* choice silver: the heart of the wicked *is* little worth.

The lips of the righteous feed many: but fools die for want of wisdom.

Proverbs 10:31,32

The mouth of the just bringeth forth wisdom: but the froward tongue shall be cut out.

The lips of the righteous know what is acceptable: but the mouth of the wicked *speaketh* frowardness.

Proverbs 11:11

By the blessing of the upright the city is exalted: but it is overthrown by the mouth of the wicked.

Proverbs 12:13

The wicked is snared by the transgression of *his* lips: but the just shall come out of trouble.

Proverbs 12:14

A man shall be satisfied with good by the fruit of *his* mouth: and the recompense of a man's hands shall be rendered unto him.

Proverbs 12:18

There is that speaketh like the piercings of a sword: but the tongue of the wise *is* health.

Proverbs 13:2

A man shall eat good by the fruit of *his* mouth: but the soul of the transgressors *shall eat* violence.

Proverbs 13:3

He that keepeth his mouth keepeth his life: *but* he that openeth wide his lips shall have destruction.

Proverbs 14:3

In the mouth of the foolish *is* a rod of pride: but the lips of the wise shall preserve them.

Proverbs 14:23

In all labour there is profit: but the talk of the lips *tendeth* only to penury.

Proverbs 15:1

A soft answer turneth away wrath: but grievous words stir up anger.

Proverbs 15:2

The tongue of the wise useth knowledge aright: but the mouth of fools poureth out foolishness.

Proverbs 15:4

A wholesome tongue *is* a tree of life: but perverseness therein *is* a breach in the spirit.

Proverbs 15:7

The lips of the wise disperse knowledge: but the heart of the foolish *doeth* not so.

Proverbs 15:23

A man hath joy by the answer of his mouth: and a word *spoken* in due season, how good *is it!*

Proverbs 15:26

The thoughts of the wicked *are* an abomination to the Lord: but *the words* of the pure *are* pleasant words.

Proverbs 15:28

The heart of the righteous studieth to answer: but the mouth of the wicked poureth out evil things.

Proverbs 16:1

The preparations of the heart in man, and the answer of the tongue, *is* from the Lord.

Proverbs 16:13

Righteous lips *are* the delight of kings; and they love him that speaketh right.

Proverbs 16:21

The wise in heart shall be called prudent: and the sweetness of the lips increaseth learning.

Proverbs 16:24

Pleasant words *are as* an honeycomb, sweet to the soul, and health to the bones.

Proverbs 16:27

An ungodly man diggeth up evil: and in his lips *there is* as a burning fire.

Proverbs 17:7

Excellent speech becometh not a fool: much less do lying lips a prince.

Proverbs 17:20

He that hath a froward heart findeth no good: and he that hath a perverse tongue falleth into mischief.

Proverbs 17:27

He that hath knowledge spareth his words: *and* a man of understanding is of an excellent spirit.

Proverbs 17:28

Even a fool, when he holdeth his peace, is counted wise: *and* he that shutteth his lips *is esteemed* a man of understanding.

Proverbs 18:6

A fool's lips enter into contention, and his mouth calleth for strokes.

Proverbs 18:7

A fool's mouth *is* his destruction, and his lips *are* the snare of his soul.

Proverbs 18:20

A man's belly shall be satisfied with the fruit of his mouth; *and* with the increase of his lips shall he be filled.

Proverbs 18:21

Death and life *are* in the power of the tongue: and they that love it shall eat the fruit thereof.

Proverbs 19:1

Better *is* the poor that walketh in his integrity, than *he that is* perverse in his lips, and is a fool.

Proverbs 21:9; 25:24

It is better to dwell in a corner of the housetop, than with a brawling woman in a wide house.

Proverbs 21:23

Whoso keepeth his mouth and his tongue keepeth his soul from troubles.

Proverbs 23:9

Speak not in the ears of a fool: for he will despise the wisdom of thy words.

Proverbs 24:26

Every man shall kiss *his* lips that giveth a right answer.

Proverbs 25:11

A word fitly spoken *is like* apples of gold in pictures of silver.

Proverbs 26:22

The words of a talebearer *are* as wounds, and they go down into the innermost parts of the belly.

Proverbs 26:23

Burning lips and a wicked heart *are like* a potsherd covered with silver dross.

Proverbs 26:28

A lying tongue hateth *those that are* afflicted by it; and a flattering mouth worketh ruin.

Proverbs 27:15

A continual dropping in a very rainy day and a contentious woman are alike.

Proverbs 29:11

A fool uttereth all his mind: but a wise *man* keepeth it in till afterwards.

Proverbs 29:20

Seest thou a man *that is* hasty in his words? *there is* more hope of a fool than of him.

EVIL SPEAKING

Proverbs 2:11-14

Discretion shall preserve thee, understanding shall keep thee:

To deliver thee from the way of the evil *man*, from the man that speaketh froward things;

Who leave the paths of uprightness, to walk in the ways of darkness;

Who rejoice to do evil, *and* delight in the frowardness of the wicked.

Proverbs 4:24

Put away from thee a froward mouth, and perverse lips put far from thee.

Proverbs 6:12

A naughty person, a wicked man, walketh with a froward mouth.

Proverbs 8:13

The fear of the Lord *is* to hate evil: pride, and arrogancy, and the evil way, and the froward mouth, do I hate.

Proverbs 10:18

He that hideth hatred *with* lying lips, and he that uttereth a slander, *is* a fool.

Proverbs 30:32

If thou hast done foolishly in lifting up thyself, or if thou hast thought evil, *lay* thine hand upon thy mouth.

FLATTERY

Proverbs 20:19

He that goeth about *as* a talebearer revealeth secrets: therefore meddle not with him that flattereth with his lips.

Proverbs 26:28

A lying tongue hateth *those that are* afflicted by it; and a flattering mouth worketh ruin.

Proverbs 28:23

He that rebuketh a man afterwards shall find more favour than he that flattereth with the tongue.

Proverbs 29:5

A man that flattereth his neighbour spreadeth a net for his feet.

GOSSIP

Proverbs 6:16,19

These six *things* doth the Lord hate: yea, seven *are* an abomination unto him:

A false witness *that* speaketh lies, and he that soweth discord among brethren.

Proverbs 10:12

Hatred stirreth up strifes: but love covereth all sins.

Proverbs 11:9

An hypocrite with *his* mouth destroyeth his neighbour: but through knowledge shall the just be delivered.

Proverbs 11:12

He that is void of wisdom despiseth his neighbour: but a man of understanding holdeth his peace.

Proverbs 11:13

A talebearer revealeth secrets: but he that is of a faithful spirit concealeth the matter.

Proverbs 16:27

An ungodly man diggeth up evil: and in his lips *there is* as a burning fire.

Proverbs 16:28

A froward man soweth strife: and a whisperer separateth chief friends.

Proverbs 17:9

He that covereth a transgression seeketh love; but he that repeateth a matter separateth *very* friends.

Proverbs 18:8; 26:22

The words of a talebearer *are* as wounds, and they go down into the innermost parts of the belly.

Proverbs 20:19

He that goeth about *as* a talebearer revealeth secrets: therefore meddle not with him that flattereth with his lips.

Proverbs 25:9,10

Debate thy cause with thy neighbour *himself*; and discover not a secret to another:

Lest he that heareth *it* put thee to shame, and thine infamy turn not away.

Proverbs 25:23

The north wind driveth away rain: so *doth* an angry
countenance a backbiting tongue.

Proverbs 26:20

Where no wood is, *there* the fire goeth out: so where
there is no talebearer, the strife ceaseth.

LYING

Proverbs 6:16,17,19

These six *things* doth the Lord hate: yea, seven *are* an abomination unto him:

A proud look, a lying tongue, and hands that shed innocent blood,

A false witness *that* speaketh lies, and he that soweth discord among brethren.

Proverbs 12:17

He that speaketh truth sheweth forth righteousness: but a false witness deceit.

Proverbs 12:19

The lip of truth shall be established for ever: but a lying tongue *is* but for a moment.

Proverbs 12:20

Deceit *is* in the heart of them that imagine evil: but to the counsellers of peace *is* joy.

Proverbs 12:22

Lying lips *are* abomination to the Lord: but they that deal truly *are* his delight.

Proverbs 13:5

A righteous *man* hateth lying: but a wicked *man* is loathsome, and cometh to shame.

Proverbs 14:5

A faithful witness will not lie: but a false witness will utter lies.

Proverbs 14:25

A true witness delivereth souls: but a deceitful *witness* speaketh lies.

Proverbs 17:4

A wicked doer giveth heed to false lips; *and* a liar giveth ear to a naughty tongue.

Proverbs 17:7

Excellent speech becometh not a fool: much less do lying lips a prince.

Proverbs 19:5

A false witness shall not be unpunished, and *he that* speaketh lies shall not escape.

Proverbs 19:9

A false witness shall not be unpunished, and *he that* speaketh lies shall perish.

Proverbs 19:22

The desire of a man *is* his kindness: and a poor man *is* better than a liar.

Proverbs 20:17

Bread of deceit *is* sweet to a man; but afterwards his mouth shall be filled with gravel.

Proverbs 21:6

The getting of treasures by a lying tongue *is* a vanity tossed to and fro of them that seek death.

Proverbs 21:28

A false witness shall perish: but the man that heareth speaketh constantly.

Proverbs 24:28,29

Be not a witness against thy neighbour without cause; and deceive *not* with thy lips.

Say not, I will do so to him as he hath done to me: I will render to the man according to his work.

Proverbs 25:14

Whoso boasteth himself of a false gift *is like* clouds and wind without rain.

Proverbs 25:18

A man that beareth false witness against his neighbour *is* a maul, and a sword, and a sharp arrow.

Proverbs 26:18,19

As a mad *man* who casteth firebrands, arrows and death,

So *is* the man *that* deceiveth his neighbour, and saith, Am not I in sport?

Proverbs 26:28

A lying tongue hateth *those that are* afflicted by it; and a flattering mouth worketh ruin.

Proverbs 28:13

He that covereth his sins shall not prosper: but whoso confesseth and forsaketh *them* shall have mercy.

Proverbs 30:5,6

Every word of God *is* pure: he *is* a shield unto them that put their trust in him.

Add thou not unto his words, lest he reprove thee, and thou be found a liar.

TATTLETALES

Proverbs 10:12

Hatred stirreth up strifes: but love covereth all sins.

Proverbs 17:9

He that covereth a transgression seeketh love; but he that repeateth a matter separateth *very* friends.

Proverbs 19:11

The discretion of a man deferreth his anger; and *it is* his glory to pass over a transgression.

Proverbs 25:9,10

Debate thy cause with thy neighbour *himself*; and discover not a secret to another:

Lest he that heareth *it* put thee to shame, and thine infamy turn not away.

TEASING

Proverbs 3:30

Strive not with a man without cause, if he have done thee no harm.

Proverbs 10:23

It is as sport to a fool to do mischief: but a man of understanding hath wisdom.

Proverbs 26:18,19

As a mad *man* who casteth firebrands, arrows and death,

So *is* the man *that* deceiveth his neighbour, and saith, Am not I in sport?

PART FIVE

Relationships

AVOIDING BAD ASSOCIATIONS

Proverbs 1:10,15

My son, if sinners entice thee, consent thou not.

My son, walk not thou in the way with them; refrain thy foot from their path.

Proverbs 2:10-12,20

When wisdom entereth into thine heart, and knowledge is pleasant unto thy soul;

Discretion shall preserve thee, understanding shall keep thee:

To deliver thee from the way of the evil *man*, from the man that speaketh froward things;

That thou mayest walk in the way of good *men*, and keep the paths of the righteous.

Proverbs 4:14,15

Enter not into the path of the wicked, and go not in the way of evil *men.*

Avoid it, pass not by it, turn from it, and pass away.

Proverbs 9:6

Forsake the foolish, and live; and go in the way of understanding.

Proverbs 12:11

He that tilleth his land shall be satisfied with bread: but he that followeth vain *persons is* void of understanding.

Proverbs 13:20

He that walketh with wise *men* shall be wise: but a companion of fools shall be destroyed.

Proverbs 14:7

Go from the presence of a foolish man, when thou perceivest not *in him* the lips of knowledge.

Proverbs 14:16

A wise *man* feareth, and departeth from evil: but the fool rageth, and is confident.

Proverbs 16:17

The highway of the upright *is* to depart from evil: he that keepeth his way preserveth his soul.

Proverbs 16:19

Better *it is to be* of an humble spirit with the lowly, than to divide the spoil with the proud.

Proverbs 16:29

A violent man enticeth his neighbour, and leadeth him into the way *that is* not good.

Proverbs 19:27

Cease, my son, to hear the instruction *that causeth* to err from the words of knowledge.

Proverbs 20:19

He that goeth about *as* a talebearer revealeth secrets: therefore meddle not with him that flattereth with his lips.

Proverbs 22:5

Thorns *and* snares *are* in the way of the froward: he that doth keep his soul shall be far from them.

Proverbs 22:24,25

Make no friendship with an angry man; and with a furious man thou shalt not go:

Lest thou learn his ways, and get a snare to thy soul.

Proverbs 23:6,7

Eat thou not the bread of *him that hath* an evil eye, neither desire thou his dainty meats:

For as he thinketh in his heart, so *is* he: Eat and drink, saith he to thee; but his heart *is* not with thee.

Proverbs 23:20,21

Be not among wine-bibbers; among riotous eaters of flesh:

For the drunkard and the glutton shall come to poverty: and drowsiness shall clothe *a man* with rags.

Proverbs 24:1

Be not thou envious against evil men, neither desire to be with them.

Proverbs 28:4

They that forsake the law praise the wicked: but such as keep the law contend with them.

Proverbs 28:7

Whoso keepeth the law *is* a wise son: but he that is a companion of riotous *men* shameth his father.

Proverbs 28:19

He that tilleth his land shall have plenty of bread: but he that followeth after vain *persons* shall have poverty enough.

Proverbs 29:24

Whoso is partner with a thief hateth his own soul: he heareth cursing, and bewrayeth *it* not.

Proverbs 29:27

An unjust man *is* an abomination to the just: and *he that is* upright in the way *is* abomination to the wicked.

BUSYBODY

Proverbs 20:3

It is an honour for a man to cease from strife: but every fool will be meddling.

Proverbs 26:17

He that passeth by, *and* meddleth with strife *belonging* not to him, *is like* one that taketh a dog by the ears.

CONFRONTING

Proverbs 9:8

Reprove not a scorner, lest he hate thee: rebuke a wise man, and he will love thee.

Proverbs 24:24,25

He that saith unto the wicked, Thou *art* righteous; him shall the people curse, nations shall abhor him:

But to them that rebuke *him* shall be delight, and a good blessing shall come upon them.

Proverbs 25:9,10

Debate thy cause with thy neighbour *himself*; and discover not a secret to another:

Lest he that heareth *it* put thee to shame, and thine infamy turn not away.

Proverbs 25:11

A word fitly spoken *is like* apples of gold in pictures of silver.

Proverbs 25:12

As an earring of gold, and an ornament of fine gold, *so* *is* a wise reprover upon an obedient ear.

Proverbs 26:17

He that passeth by, *and* meddleth with strife *belonging* not to him, *is like* one that taketh a dog by the ears.

Proverbs 27:17

Iron sharpeneth iron; so a man sharpeneth the countenance of his friend.

Proverbs 28:4

They that forsake the law praise the wicked: but such as keep the law contend with them.

Proverbs 28:13

He that covereth his sins shall not prosper: but whoso confesseth and forsaketh *them* shall have mercy.

Proverbs 28:23

He that rebuketh a man afterwards shall find more favour than he that flattereth with the tongue.

Proverbs 29:27

An unjust man *is* an abomination to the just: and *he* *that is* upright in the way *is* abomination to the wicked.

COUNSEL AND ADVICE

Proverbs 1:5

A wise *man* will hear, and will increase learning; and a man of understanding shall attain unto wise counsels.

Proverbs 11:14

Where no counsel *is*, the people fall: but in the multitude of counsellers *there is* safety.

Proverbs 12:5

The thoughts of the righteous *are* right: *but* the counsels of the wicked *are* deceit.

Proverbs 12:15

The way of a fool *is* right in his own eyes: but he that hearkeneth unto counsel *is* wise.

Proverbs 12:20

Deceit *is* in the heart of them that imagine evil: but to the counsellers of peace *is* joy.

Proverbs 13:10

Only by pride cometh contention: but with the well advised *is* wisdom.

Proverbs 15:22

Without counsel purposes are disappointed: but in the multitude of counsellers they are established.

Proverbs 18:13

He that answereth a matter before he heareth *it*, it *is* folly and shame unto him.

Proverbs 19:20

Hear counsel, and receive instruction, that thou mayest be wise in thy latter end.

Proverbs 19:21

There are many devices in a man's heart; nevertheless the counsel of the Lord, that shall stand.

Proverbs 20:5

Counsel in the heart of man *is like* deep water; but a man of understanding will draw it out.

Proverbs 20:18

Every purpose is established by counsel: and with good advice make war.

Proverbs 21:30

There is no wisdom nor understanding nor counsel against the Lord.

Proverbs 24:6

For by wise counsel thou shalt make thy war: and in multitude of counsellors *there is* safety.

Proverbs 25:19

Confidence in an unfaithful man in time of trouble *is like* a broken tooth, and a foot out of joint.

Proverbs 27:9

Ointment and perfume rejoice the heart: so *doth* the sweetness of a man's friend by hearty counsel.

Proverbs 27:17

Iron sharpeneth iron; so a man sharpeneth the countenance of his friend.

GETTING ALONG WITH OTHERS

Proverbs 3:28

Say not unto thy neighbour, Go, and come again, and to morrow I will give; when thou hast it by thee.

Proverbs 3:29

Devise not evil against thy neighbour, seeing he dwelleth securely by thee.

Proverbs 3:30

Strive not with a man without cause, if he have done thee no harm.

Proverbs 11:12

He that is void of wisdom despiseth his neighbour: but a man of understanding holdeth his peace.

Proverbs 16:7

When a man's ways please the Lord, he maketh even his enemies to be at peace with him.

Proverbs 24:28

Be not a witness against thy neighbour without cause; and deceive *not* with thy lips.

Proverbs 25:9

Debate thy cause with thy neighbour *himself*; and discover not a secret to another.

Proverbs 25:17

Withdraw thy foot from thy neighbour's house; lest he be weary of thee, and *so* hate thee.

Proverbs 25:18

A man that beareth false witness against his neighbour *is* a maul, and a sword, and a sharp arrow.

Proverbs 25:20

As he that taketh away a garment in cold weather, *and as* vinegar upon nitre, so *is* he that singeth songs to an heavy heart.

Proverbs 25:21,22

If thine enemy be hungry, give him bread to eat; and if he be thirsty, give him water to drink:

For thou shalt heap coals of fire upon his head, and the Lord shall reward thee.

Proverbs 26:18,19

As a mad *man* who casteth firebrands, arrows and death,

So *is* the man *that* deceiveth his neighbour, and saith,
Am not I in sport?

Proverbs 27:14

He that blesseth his friend with a loud voice, rising early
in the morning, it shall be counted a curse to him.

GOVERNMENT BLESSED

Proverbs 11:10

When it goeth well with the righteous, the city rejoiceth: and when the wicked perish, *there is* shouting.

Proverbs 11:11

By the blessing of the upright the city is exalted: but it is overthrown by the mouth of the wicked.

Proverbs 14:34

Righteousness exalteth a nation: but sin *is* a reproach to any people.

Proverbs 16:12

It is an abomination to kings to commit wickedness: for the throne is established by righteousness.

Proverbs 16:13

Righteous lips *are* the delight of kings; and they love him that speaketh right.

Proverbs 20:8

A king that sitteth in the throne of judgment scattereth away all evil with his eyes.

Proverbs 20:28

Mercy and truth preserve the king: and his throne is upholden by mercy.

Proverbs 25:5

Take away the wicked *from* before the king, and his throne shall be established in righteousness.

Proverbs 28:2

For the transgression of a land many *are* the princes thereof: but by a man of understanding *and* knowledge the state *thereof* shall be prolonged.

Proverbs 29:2

When the righteous are in authority, the people rejoice: but when the wicked beareth rule, the people mourn.

Proverbs 29:8

Scornful men bring a city into a snare: but wise *men* turn away wrath.

Proverbs 29:14

The king that faithfully judgeth the poor, his throne shall be established for ever.

LOVE AND FRIENDSHIP

Proverbs 10:12

Hatred stirreth up strifes: but love covereth all sins.

Proverbs 15:17

Better *is* a dinner of herbs where love is, than a stalled ox and hatred therewith.

Proverbs 16:7

When a man's ways please the Lord, he maketh even his enemies to be at peace with him.

Proverbs 17:9

He that covereth a transgression seeketh love; but he that repeateth a matter separateth *very* friends.

Proverbs 17:17

A friend loveth at all times, and a brother is born for adversity.

Proverbs 18:19

A brother offended *is harder to be won* than a strong
city: and *their* contentions *are* like the bars of a castle.

Proverbs 18:24

A man *that hath* friends must shew himself friendly: and
there is a friend *that* sticketh closer than a brother.

Proverbs 22:24

Make no friendship with an angry man; and with a
furious man thou shalt not go.

Proverbs 27:6

Faithful *are* the wounds of a friend; but the kisses of an
enemy *are* deceitful.

Proverbs 27:9

Ointment and perfume rejoice the heart: so *doth* the
sweetness of a man's friend by hearty counsel.

Proverbs 27:10

Thine own friend, and thy father's friend, forsake not;
neither go into thy brother's house in the day of thy
calamity: *for* better *is* a neighbour *that is* near than a
brother far off.

Proverbs 27:17

Iron sharpeneth iron; so a man sharpeneth the countenance of his friend.

RESPECT OF PARENTS

Proverbs 1:8,9

My son, hear the instruction of thy father, and forsake not the law of thy mother:

For they *shall be* an ornament of grace unto thy head, and chains about thy neck.

Proverbs 4:1,2

Hear, ye children, the instruction of a father, and attend to know understanding.

For I give you good doctrine, forsake ye not my law.

Proverbs 4:10-12

Hear, O my son, and receive my sayings; and the years of thy life shall be many.

I have taught thee in the way of wisdom; I have led thee in right paths.

When thou goest, thy steps shall not be straitened; and when thou runnest, thou shalt not stumble.

Proverbs 4:20-22

My son, attend to my words; incline thine ear unto my sayings.

Let them not depart from thine eyes; keep them in the midst of thine heart.

For they *are* life unto those that find them, and health to all their flesh.

Proverbs 6:20-23

My son, keep thy father's commandment, and forsake not the law of thy mother:

Bind them continually upon thine heart, *and* tie them about thy neck.

When thou goest, it shall lead thee; when thou sleepest, it shall keep thee; and *when* thou awakest, it shall talk with thee.

For the commandment *is* a lamp; and the law *is* light; and reproofs of instruction *are* the way of life:

Proverbs 7:1-3

My son, keep my words, and lay up my commandments with thee.

Keep my commandments, and live; and my law as the apple of thine eye.

Bind them upon thy fingers, write them upon the table of thine heart.

Proverbs 10:1

The proverbs of Solomon. A wise son maketh a glad father: but a foolish son *is* the heaviness of his mother.

Proverbs 13:1

A wise son *heareth* his father's instruction: but a scorner heareth not rebuke.

Proverbs 15:5

A fool despiseth his father's instruction: but he that regardeth reproof is prudent.

Proverbs 15:20

A wise son maketh a glad father: but a foolish man despiseth his mother.

Proverbs 17:6

Children's children *are* the crown of old men; and the glory of children *are* their fathers.

Proverbs 19:26

He that wasteth *his* father, *and* chaseth away *his* mother, *is* a son that causeth shame, and bringeth reproach.

Proverbs 20:20

Whoso curseth his father or his mother, his lamp shall be put out in obscure darkness.

Proverbs 23:22

Hearken unto thy father that begat thee, and despise not thy mother when she is old.

Proverbs 23:24,25

The father of the righteous shall greatly rejoice: and he that begetteth a wise *child* shall have joy of him.

Thy father and thy mother shall be glad, and she that bare thee shall rejoice.

Proverbs 23:26

My son, give me thine heart, and let thine eyes observe my ways.

Proverbs 28:7

Whoso keepeth the law *is* a wise son: but he that is a companion of riotous *men* shameth his father.

Proverbs 28:24

Whoso robbeth his father or his mother, and saith, *It is* no transgression; the same *is* the companion of a destroyer.

Proverbs 30:17

The eye *that* mocketh at *his* father and despiseth to obey *his* mother, the ravens of the valley shall pick it out, and the young eagles shall eat it.

PART SIX

Wrong Doings

BRIBERY

Proverbs 15:27

He that is greedy of gain troubleth his own house; but
he that hateth gifts shall live.

Proverbs 17:23

A wicked *man* taketh a gift out of the bosom to pervert
the ways of judgment.

Proverbs 17:26

Also to punish the just *is* not good, *nor* to strike princes
for equity.

Proverbs 28:21

To have respect of persons *is* not good: for for a piece
of bread *that* man will transgress.

Proverbs 29:4

The king by judgment establisheth the land: but he that
receiveth gifts overthroweth it.

CHEATING AND STEALING

Proverbs 6:30

Men do not despise a thief, if he steal to satisfy his soul when he is hungry.

Proverbs 11:1

A false balance *is* abomination to the Lord: but a just weight *is* his delight.

Proverbs 12:22

Lying lips *are* abomination to the Lord: but they that deal truly *are* his delight.

Proverbs 16:8

Better *is* a little with righteousness than great revenues without right.

Proverbs 20:23

Divers weights *are* an abomination unto the Lord; and a false balance *is* not good.

Proverbs 21:7

The robbery of the wicked shall destroy them; because they refuse to do judgment.

Proverbs 28:8

He that by usury and unjust gain increaseth his substance, he shall gather it for him that will pity the poor.

Proverbs 29:24

Whoso is partner with a thief hateth his own soul: he heareth cursing, and bewrayeth *it* not.

CRUELTY

Proverbs 11:17

The merciful man doeth good to his own soul: but *he that is* cruel troubleth his own flesh.

Proverbs 12:10

A righteous *man* regardeth the life of his beast: but the tender mercies of the wicked *are* cruel.

Proverbs 17:11

An evil *man* seeketh only rebellion: therefore a cruel messenger shall be sent against him.

Proverbs 27:4

Wrath *is* cruel, and anger *is* outrageous; but who *is* able to stand before envy?

EVIL

Proverbs 1:10,15,16

My son, if sinners entice thee, consent thou not.

My son, walk not thou in the way with them; refrain thy foot from their path:

For their feet run to evil, and make haste to shed blood.

Proverbs 2:11-14

Discretion shall preserve thee, understanding shall keep thee:

To deliver thee from the way of the evil *man*, from the man that speaketh froward things;

Who leave the paths of uprightness, to walk in the ways of darkness;

Who rejoice to do evil, *and* delight in the frowardness of the wicked.

Proverbs 3:7

Be not wise in thine own eyes: fear the Lord, and depart from evil.

Proverbs 4:14-17

Enter not into the path of the wicked, and go not in the way of evil *men.*

Avoid it, pass not by it, turn from it, and pass away.

For they sleep not, except they have done mischief; and their sleep is taken away, unless they cause *some* to fall.

For they eat the bread of wickedness, and drink the wine of violence.

Proverbs 4:27

Turn not to the right hand nor to the left: remove thy foot from evil.

Proverbs 8:13

The fear of the Lord *is* to hate evil: pride, and arrogancy, and the evil way, and the froward mouth, do I hate.

Proverbs 12:21

There shall no evil happen to the just: but the wicked shall be filled with mischief.

Proverbs 13:21

Evil pursueth sinners: but to the righteous good shall be repayed.

Proverbs 14:16

A wise *man* feareth, and departeth from evil: but the fool rageth, and is confident.

Proverbs 14:19

The evil bow before the good; and the wicked at the gates of the righteous.

Proverbs 15:3

The eyes of the Lord *are* in every place, beholding the evil and the good.

Proverbs 15:15

All the days of the afflicted *are* evil: but he that is of a merry heart *hath* a continual feast.

Proverbs 16:6

By mercy and truth iniquity is purged: and by the fear of the Lord *men* depart from evil.

Proverbs 16:17

The highway of the upright *is* to depart from evil: he that keepeth his way preserveth his soul.

Proverbs 16:27

An ungodly man diggeth up evil: and in his lips *there is* as a burning fire.

Proverbs 16:29,30

A violent man enticeth his neighbour, and leadeth him into the way *that is* not good.

He shutteth his eyes to devise froward things: moving his lips he bringeth evil to pass.

Proverbs 17:11

An evil *man* seeketh only rebellion: therefore a cruel messenger shall be sent against him.

Proverbs 19:23

The fear of the Lord *tendeth* to life: and *he that hath it* shall abide satisfied; he shall not be visited with evil.

Proverbs 20:8

A king that sitteth in the throne of judgment scattereth away all evil with his eyes.

Proverbs 20:22

Say not thou, I will recompense evil; *but* wait on the Lord, and he shall save thee.

Proverbs 21:10

The soul of the wicked desireth evil: his neighbour findeth no favour in his eyes.

Proverbs 22:3; 27:12

A prudent *man* foreseeth the evil and hideth himself: but the simple pass on; and are punished.

Proverbs 24:20

For there shall be no reward to the evil *man*; the candle of the wicked shall be put out.

Proverbs 28:5

Evil men understand not judgment: but they that seek the Lord understand all *things*.

Proverbs 29:6

In the transgression of an evil man *there is* a snare: but the righteous doth sing and rejoice.

EVIL PLANNING

Proverbs 3:29

Devise not evil against thy neighbour, seeing he dwelleth securely by thee.

Proverbs 11:19

As righteousness *tendeth* to life: so he that pursueth evil *pursueth it* to his own death.

Proverbs 11:27

He that diligently seeketh good procureth favour: but he that seeketh mischief, it shall come unto him.

Proverbs 12:2

A good *man* obtaineth favour of the Lord: but a man of wicked devices will he condemn.

Proverbs 12:3

A man shall not be established by wickedness: but the root of the righteous shall not be moved.

Proverbs 14:22

Do they not err that devise evil? but mercy and truth *shall be* to them that devise good.

Proverbs 17:13

Whoso rewardeth evil for good, evil shall not depart from his house.

Proverbs 20:22

Say not thou, I will recompense evil; *but* wait on the Lord, and he shall save thee.

Proverbs 22:8

He that soweth iniquity shall reap vanity: and the rod of his anger shall fail.

Proverbs 24:8

He that deviseth to do evil shall be called a mischievous person.

Proverbs 24:28,29

Be not a witness against thy neighbour without cause; and deceive *not* with thy lips.

Say not, I will do so to him as he hath done to me: I will render to the man according to his work.

Proverbs 25:21,22

If thine enemy be hungry, give him bread to eat; and if he be thirsty, give him water to drink:

For thou shalt heap coals of fire upon his head, and the Lord shall reward thee.

Proverbs 28:10

Whoso causeth the righteous to go astray in an evil way, he shall fall himself into his own pit: but the upright shall have good *things* in possession.

EVIL THINKING

Proverbs 6:16,18

These six *things* doth the Lord hate: yea, seven *are* an abomination unto him:

An heart that deviseth wicked imaginations, feet that be swift in running to mischief.

Proverbs 12:20

Deceit *is* in the heart of them that imagine evil: but to the counsellers of peace *is* joy.

Proverbs 30:32

If thou hast done foolishly in lifting up thyself, or if thou hast thought evil, *lay* thine hand upon thy mouth.

MISCHIEF

Proverbs 6:16,18

These six *things* doth the Lord hate: yea, seven *are* an abomination unto him:

An heart that deviseth wicked imaginations, feet that be swift in running to mischief.

Proverbs 10:23

It is as sport to a fool to do mischief: but a man of understanding hath wisdom.

Proverbs 11:27

He that diligently seeketh good procureth favour: but he that seeketh mischief, it shall come unto him.

Proverbs 12:21

There shall no evil happen to the just: but the wicked shall be filled with mischief.

Proverbs 13:17

A wicked messenger falleth into mischief: but a faithful ambassador *is* health.

Proverbs 15:21

Folly *is* joy to *him that is* destitute of wisdom: but a man of understanding walketh uprightly.

Proverbs 17:20

He that hath a froward heart findeth no good: and he that hath a perverse tongue falleth into mischief.

Proverbs 24:1,2

Be not thou envious against evil men, neither desire to be with them.

For their heart studieth destruction, and their lips talk of mischief.

Proverbs 24:8

He that deviseth to do evil shall be called a mischievous person.

Proverbs 24:16

For a just *man* falleth seven times, and riseth up again: but the wicked shall fall into mischief.

Proverbs 26:18,19

As a mad *man* who casteth firebrands, arrows and death,

So *is* the man *that* deceiveth his neighbour, and saith, Am not I in sport?

Proverbs 28:14

Happy *is* the man that feareth alway: but he that hardeneth his heart shall fall into mischief.

REJOICING IN EVIL

Proverbs 17:5

Whoso mocketh the poor reproacheth his Maker: *and* he that is glad at calamities shall not be unpunished.

Proverbs 24:17,18

Rejoice not when thine enemy falleth, and let not thine heart be glad when he stumbleth:

Lest the Lord see *it*, and it displease him, and he turn away his wrath from him.

SCORN

Proverbs 3:34

Surely he scorneth the scorners: but he giveth grace unto the lowly.

Proverbs 9:12

If thou be wise, thou shalt be wise for thyself: but *if* thou scornest, thou alone shalt bear *it*.

Proverbs 12:6

The words of the wicked *are* to lie in wait for blood: but the mouth of the upright shall deliver them.

Proverbs 13:1

A wise son *heareth* his father's instruction: but a scorner heareth not rebuke.

Proverbs 14:6

A scorner seeketh wisdom, and *findeth it* not: but knowledge *is* easy unto him that understandeth.

Proverbs 15:12

A scorner loveth not one that reproveth him: neither
will he go unto the wise.

Proverbs 19:25

Smite a scorner, and the simple will beware: and reprove one that hath understanding, *and* he will understand knowledge.

Proverbs 19:28

An ungodly witness scorneth judgment: and the mouth
of the wicked devoureth iniquity.

Proverbs 19:29

Judgments are prepared for scorners, and stripes for the
back of fools.

Proverbs 21:11

When the scorner is punished, the simple is made wise:
and when the wise is instructed, he receiveth knowledge.

Proverbs 22:10

Cast out the scorner, and contention shall go out; yea,
strife and reproach shall cease.

Proverbs 24:9

The thought of foolishness *is* sin: and the scorner *is* an abomination to men.

Proverbs 29:8

Scornful men bring a city into a snare: but wise *men* turn away wrath.

VENGEANCE

Proverbs 11:31

Behold, the righteous shall be recompensed in the earth: much more the wicked and the sinner.

Proverbs 20:22

Say not thou, I will recompense evil; *but* wait on the Lord, and he shall save thee.

Proverbs 24:28,29

Be not a witness against thy neighbour without cause; and deceive *not* with thy lips.

Say not, I will do so to him as he hath done to me: I will render to the man according to his work.

Proverbs 25:21,22

If thine enemy be hungry, give him bread to eat; and if he be thirsty, give him water to drink:

For thou shalt heap coals of fire upon his head, and the Lord shall reward thee.

WICKEDNESS

Proverbs 2:22

But the wicked shall be cut off from the earth, and the transgressors shall be rooted out of it.

Proverbs 3:33

The curse of the Lord *is* in the house of the wicked: but he blesseth the habitation of the just.

Proverbs 4:14

Enter not into the path of the wicked, and go not in the way of evil *men*.

Proverbs 4:19

The way of the wicked *is* as darkness: they know not at what they stumble.

Proverbs 5:22,23

His own iniquities shall take the wicked himself, and he shall be holden with the cords of his sins.

He shall die without instruction; and in the greatness of
his folly he shall go astray.

Proverbs 6:12-15

A naughty person, a wicked man, walketh with a froward
mouth.

He winketh with his eyes, he speaketh with his feet, he
teacheth with his fingers;

Frowardness *is* in his heart, he deviseth mischief continually; he soweth discord.

Therefore shall his calamity come suddenly; suddenly
shall he be broken without remedy.

Proverbs 10:2

Treasures of wickedness profit nothing: but righteousness delivereth from death.

Proverbs 10:3

The Lord will not suffer the soul of the righteous to famish: but he casteth away the substance of the wicked.

Proverbs 10:6

Blessings *are* upon the head of the just: but violence
covereth the mouth of the wicked.

Proverbs 10:7

The memory of the just *is* blessed: but the name of the wicked shall rot.

Proverbs 10:11

The mouth of a righteous *man is* a well of life: but violence covereth the mouth of the wicked.

Proverbs 10:16

The labour of the righteous *tendeth* to life: the fruit of the wicked to sin.

Proverbs 10:20

The tongue of the just *is as* choice silver: the heart of the wicked *is* little worth.

Proverbs 10:24

The fear of the wicked, it shall come upon him: but the desire of the righteous shall be granted.

Proverbs 10:25

As the whirlwind passeth, so *is* the wicked no *more*: but the righteous *is* an everlasting foundation.

Proverbs 10:27

The fear of the Lord prolongeth days: but the years of the wicked shall be shortened.

Proverbs 10:28

The hope of the righteous *shall be* gladness: but the expectation of the wicked shall perish.

Proverbs 10:29

The way of the Lord *is* strength to the upright: but destruction *shall be* to the workers of iniquity.

Proverbs 10:30

The righteous shall never be removed: but the wicked shall not inhabit the earth.

Proverbs 10:32

The lips of the righteous know what is acceptable: but the mouth of the wicked *speaketh* frowardness.

Proverbs 11:5

The righteousness of the perfect shall direct his way: but the wicked shall fall by his own wickedness.

Proverbs 11:7

When a wicked man dieth, *his* expectation shall perish: and the hope of unjust *men* perisheth.

Proverbs 11:8

The righteous is delivered out of trouble, and the wicked cometh in his stead.

Proverbs 11:11

By the blessing of the upright the city is exalted: but it is overthrown by the mouth of the wicked.

Proverbs 11:18

The wicked worketh a deceitful work: but to him that soweth righteousness *shall be* a sure reward.

Proverbs 11:21

Though hand *join* in hand, the wicked shall not be unpunished: but the seed of the righteous shall be delivered.

Proverbs 11:23

The desire of the righteous *is* only good: *but* the expectation of the wicked *is* wrath.

Proverbs 11:31

Behold, the righteous shall be recompensed in the earth: much more the wicked and the sinner.

Proverbs 12:2

A good *man* obtaineth favour of the Lord: but a man of wicked devices will he condemn.

Proverbs 12:3

A man shall not be established by wickedness: but the root of the righteous shall not be moved.

Proverbs 12:5

The thoughts of the righteous *are* right: *but* the counsels of the wicked *are* deceit.

Proverbs 12:6

The words of the wicked *are* to lie in wait for blood: but the mouth of the upright shall deliver them.

Proverbs 12:7

The wicked are overthrown, and *are* not: but the house of the righteous shall stand.

Proverbs 12:10

A righteous *man* regardeth the life of his beast: but the tender mercies of the wicked *are* cruel.

Proverbs 12:12

The wicked desireth the net of evil *men*: but the root of the righteous yieldeth *fruit*.

Proverbs 12:13

The wicked is snared by the transgression of *his* lips: but the just shall come out of trouble.

Proverbs 12:21

There shall no evil happen to the just: but the wicked shall be filled with mischief.

Proverbs 12:26

The righteous *is* more excellent than his neighbour: but the way of the wicked seduceth them.

Proverbs 13:5

A righteous *man* hateth lying: but a wicked *man* is loathsome, and cometh to shame.

Proverbs 13:6

Righteousness keepeth *him that is* upright in the way: but wickedness overthroweth the sinner.

Proverbs 13:9

The light of the righteous rejoiceth: but the lamp of the wicked shall be put out.

Proverbs 13:25

The righteous eateth to the satisfying of his soul: but the belly of the wicked shall want.

Proverbs 14:11

The house of the wicked shall be overthrown: but the tabernacle of the upright shall flourish.

Proverbs 14:19

The evil bow before the good; and the wicked at the gates of the righteous.

Proverbs 14:32

The wicked is driven away in his wickedness: but the righteous hath hope in his death.

Proverbs 15:6

In the house of the righteous *is* much treasure: but in the revenues of the wicked is trouble.

Proverbs 15:8

The sacrifice of the wicked *is* an abomination to the Lord: but the prayer of the upright *is* his delight.

Proverbs 15:9

The way of the wicked *is* an abomination unto the Lord: but he loveth him that followeth after righteousness.

Proverbs 15:26

The thoughts of the wicked *are* an abomination to the Lord: but *the words* of the pure *are* pleasant words.

Proverbs 15:28

The heart of the righteous studieth to answer: but the mouth of the wicked poureth out evil things.

Proverbs 15:29

The Lord *is* far from the wicked: but he heareth the prayer of the righteous.

Proverbs 16:4

The Lord hath made all *things* for himself: yea, even the wicked for the day of evil.

Proverbs 16:12

It is an abomination to kings to commit wickedness: for the throne is established by righteousness.

Proverbs 17:4

A wicked doer giveth heed to false lips; *and* a liar giveth ear to a naughty tongue.

Proverbs 17:15

He that justifieth the wicked, and he that condemneth the just, even they both *are* abomination to the Lord.

Proverbs 17:23

A wicked *man* taketh a gift out of the bosom to pervert the ways of judgment.

Proverbs 18:3

When the wicked cometh, *then* cometh also contempt, and with ignominy reproach.

Proverbs 18:5

It is not good to accept the person of the wicked, to overthrow the righteous in judgment.

Proverbs 19:28

An ungodly witness scorneth judgment: and the mouth of the wicked devoureth iniquity.

Proverbs 20:26

A wise king scattereth the wicked, and bringeth the wheel over them.

Proverbs 21:4

An high look, and a proud heart, *and* the plowing of the wicked, *is* sin.

Proverbs 21:7

The robbery of the wicked shall destroy them; because they refuse to do judgment.

Proverbs 21:10

The soul of the wicked desireth evil: his neighbour findeth no favour in his eyes.

Proverbs 21:12

The righteous *man* wisely considereth the house of the wicked: *but God* overthroweth the wicked for *their* wickedness.

Proverbs 21:18

The wicked *shall be* a ransom for the righteous, and the transgressor for the upright.

Proverbs 21:27

The sacrifice of the wicked *is* abomination: how much more, *when* he bringeth it with a wicked mind?

Proverbs 21:29

A wicked man hardeneth his face: but *as for* the upright, he directeth his way.

Proverbs 24:16

For a just *man* falleth seven times, and riseth up again: but the wicked shall fall into mischief.

Proverbs 24:19,20

Fret not thyself because of evil *men*, neither be thou envious at the wicked;

For there shall be no reward to the evil *man*; the candle of the wicked shall be put out.

Proverbs 25:26

A righteous man falling down before the wicked *is as* a troubled fountain, and a corrupt spring.

Proverbs 26:23

Burning lips and a wicked heart *are like* a potsherd covered with silver dross.

Proverbs 28:1

The wicked flee when no man pursueth: but the righteous are bold as a lion.

Proverbs 28:4

They that forsake the law praise the wicked: but such as keep the law contend with them.

Proverbs 28:12

When righteous *men* do rejoice, *there is* great glory: but when the wicked rise, a man is hidden.

Proverbs 28:15

As a roaring lion, and a ranging bear; *so is* a wicked ruler over the poor people.

Proverbs 28:28

When the wicked rise, men hide themselves: but when they perish, the righteous increase.

Proverbs 29:7

The righteous considereth the cause of the poor: *but* the wicked regardeth not to know *it*.

Proverbs 29:16

When the wicked are multiplied, transgression increaseth: but the righteous shall see their fall.

Proverbs 29:27

An unjust man *is* an abomination to the just: and *he that is* upright in the way *is* abomination to the wicked.

PART SEVEN

Godly Characteristics

DISCRETION AND PRUDENCE

Proverbs 1:1,4

The proverbs of Solomon the son of David, king of Israel;

To give subtilty to the simple, to the young man knowledge and discretion.

Proverbs 2:10-12

When wisdom entereth into thine heart, and knowledge is pleasant unto thy soul;

Discretion shall preserve thee, understanding shall keep thee:

To deliver thee from the way of the evil *man*, from the man that speaketh froward things.

Proverbs 3:21

My son, let not them depart from thine eyes: keep sound wisdom and discretion.

Proverbs 5:1,2

My son, attend unto my wisdom, *and* bow thine ear to my understanding:

That thou mayest regard discretion, and *that* thy lips may keep knowledge.

Proverbs 11:22

As a jewel of gold in a swine's snout, *so is* a fair woman which is without discretion.

Proverbs 12:5

The thoughts of the righteous *are* right: *but* the counsels of the wicked *are* deceit.

Proverbs 12:16

A fool's wrath is presently known: but a prudent *man* covereth shame.

Proverbs 12:23

A prudent man concealeth knowledge: but the heart of fools proclaimeth foolishness.

Proverbs 13:16

Every prudent *man* dealeth with knowledge: but a fool layeth open *his* folly.

Proverbs 14:8

The wisdom of the prudent *is* to understand his way: but the folly of fools *is* deceit.

Proverbs 14:15

The simple believeth every word: but the prudent *man* looketh well to his going.

Proverbs 14:18

The simple inherit folly: but the prudent are crowned with knowledge.

Proverbs 15:5

A fool despiseth his father's instruction: but he that regardeth reproof is prudent.

Proverbs 16:21

The wise in heart shall be called prudent: and the sweetness of the lips increaseth learning.

Proverbs 18:15

The heart of the prudent getteth knowledge; and the ear of the wise seeketh knowledge.

Proverbs 19:11

The discretion of a man deferreth his anger; and *it is* his glory to pass over a transgression.

Proverbs 19:14

House and riches *are* the inheritance of fathers: and a prudent wife *is* from the Lord.

Proverbs 19:27

Cease, my son, to hear the instruction *that causeth* to err from the words of knowledge.

Proverbs 21:5

The thoughts of the diligent *tend* only to plenteousness; but of every one *that is* hasty only to want.

Proverbs 22:3; 27:12

A prudent *man* foreseeth the evil and hideth himself: but the simple pass on, and are punished.

FAITHFULNESS

Proverbs 11:13

A talebearer revealeth secrets: but he that is of a faithful spirit concealeth the matter.

Proverbs 13:17

A wicked messenger falleth into mischief: but a faithful ambassador *is* health.

Proverbs 14:5

A faithful witness will not lie: but a false witness will utter lies.

Proverbs 20:6

Most men will proclaim every one his own goodness: but a faithful man who can find?

Proverbs 25:13

As the cold of snow in the time of harvest, *so is* a faithful messenger to them that send him: for he refresheth the soul of his masters.

Proverbs 25:19

Confidence in an unfaithful man in time of trouble *is like* a broken tooth, and a foot out of joint.

Proverbs 28:20

A faithful man shall abound with blessings: but he that maketh haste to be rich shall not be innocent.

Proverbs 29:14

The king that faithfully judgeth the poor, his throne shall be established for ever.

GOODNESS

Proverbs 2:1,9

My son, if thou wilt receive my words, and hide my commandments with thee;

Then shalt thou understand righteousness, and judgment, and equity; *yea*, every good path.

Proverbs 3:27

Withhold not good from them to whom it is due, when it is in the power of thine hand to do *it*.

Proverbs 11:17

The merciful man doeth good to his own soul: but *he that is* cruel troubleth his own flesh.

Proverbs 11:27

He that diligently seeketh good procureth favour: but he that seeketh mischief, it shall come unto him.

Proverbs 12:2

A good *man* obtaineth favour of the Lord: but a man of wicked devices will he condemn.

Proverbs 12:25

Heaviness in the heart of man maketh it stoop: but a good word maketh it glad.

Proverbs 13:22

A good *man* leaveth an inheritance to his children's children: and the wealth of the sinner *is* laid up for the just.

Proverbs 14:14

The backslider in heart shall be filled with his own ways: and a good man *shall be satisfied* from himself.

Proverbs 14:19

The evil bow before the good; and the wicked at the gates of the righteous.

Proverbs 14:22

Do they not err that devise evil? but mercy and truth *shall be* to them that devise good.

Proverbs 16:7

When a man's ways please the Lord, he maketh even his enemies to be at peace with him.

Proverbs 16:20

He that handleth a matter wisely shall find good: and whoso trusteth in the Lord, happy *is* he.

Proverbs 17:20

He that hath a froward heart findeth no good: and he that hath a perverse tongue falleth into mischief.

Proverbs 19:8

He that getteth wisdom loveth his own soul: he that keepeth understanding shall find good.

Proverbs 22:1

A *good* name *is* rather to be chosen than great riches, *and* loving favour rather than silver and gold.

HAPPINESS

Proverbs 3:13,18

Happy *is* the man *that* findeth wisdom, and the man *that* getteth understanding.

She *is* a tree of life to them that lay hold upon her: and happy *is every one* that retaineth her.

Proverbs 12:25

Heaviness in the heart of man maketh it stoop: but a good word maketh it glad.

Proverbs 14:21

He that despiseth his neighbour sinneth: but he that hath mercy on the poor, happy *is* he.

Proverbs 15:13

A merry heart maketh a cheerful countenance: but by sorrow of the heart the spirit is broken.

Proverbs 15:15

All the days of the afflicted *are* evil: but he that is of a merry heart *hath* a continual feast.

Proverbs 16:20

He that handleth a matter wisely shall find good: and whoso trusteth in the Lord, happy *is* he.

Proverbs 17:22

A merry heart doeth good *like* a medicine: but a broken spirit drieth the bones.

Proverbs 28:14

Happy *is* the man that feareth alway: but he that hardeneth his heart shall fall into mischief.

Proverbs 29:18

Where *there is* no vision, the people perish: but he that keepeth the law, happy *is* he.

HONESTY

Proverbs 3:3

Let not mercy and truth forsake thee: bind them about thy neck; write them upon the table of thine heart.

Proverbs 11:1

A false balance *is* abomination to the Lord: but a just weight *is* his delight.

Proverbs 12:17

He that speaketh truth sheweth forth righteousness: but a false witness deceit.

Proverbs 12:19

The lip of truth shall be established for ever: but a lying tongue *is* but for a moment.

Proverbs 12:22

Lying lips *are* abomination to the Lord: but they that deal truly *are* his delight.

Proverbs 14:25

A true witness delivereth souls: but a deceitful *witness* speaketh lies.

Proverbs 16:11

A just weight and balance *are* the Lord's: all the weights of the bag *are* his work.

Proverbs 16:13

Righteous lips *are* the delight of kings; and they love him that speaketh right.

Proverbs 17:15

He that justifieth the wicked, and he that condemneth the just, even they both *are* abomination to the Lord.

Proverbs 19:1

Better *is* the poor that walketh in his integrity, than *he that is* perverse in his lips, and is a fool.

Proverbs 20:10

Divers weights, *and* divers measures, both of them *are* alike abomination to the Lord.

Proverbs 20:23

Divers weights *are* an abomination unto the Lord; and a false balance *is* not good.

Proverbs 21:3

To do justice and judgment *is* more acceptable to the Lord than sacrifice.

Proverbs 24:11,12

If thou forbear to deliver *them that are* drawn unto death, and *those that are* ready to be slain;

If thou sayest, Behold, we knew it not; doth not he that pondereth the heart consider *it?* and he that keepeth thy soul, doth *not* he know *it?* and shall *not* he render to *every* man according to his works?

Proverbs 24:28,29

Be not a witness against thy neighbour without cause; and deceive *not* with thy lips.

Say not, I will do so to him as he hath done to me: I will render to the man according to his work.

Proverbs 28:8

He that by usury and unjust gain increaseth his substance, he shall gather it for him that will pity the poor.

Proverbs 28:13

He that covereth his sins shall not prosper: but whoso
confesseth and forsaketh *them* shall have mercy.

HUMILITY

Proverbs 3:34

Surely he scorneth the scorners: but he giveth grace unto the lowly.

Proverbs 11:2

When pride cometh, then cometh shame: but with the lowly *is* wisdom.

Proverbs 15:33

The fear of the Lord *is* the instruction of wisdom; and before honour *is* humility.

Proverbs 16:19

Better *it is to be* of an humble spirit with the lowly, than to divide the spoil with the proud.

Proverbs 18:12

Before destruction the heart of man is haughty, and before honour *is* humility.

Proverbs 22:4

By humility *and* the fear of the Lord *are* riches, and honour, and life.

Proverbs 25:6,7

Put not forth thyself in the presence of the king, and stand not in the place of great *men:*

For better *it is* that it be said unto thee, Come up hither; than that thou shouldest be put lower in the presence of the prince whom thine eyes have seen.

Proverbs 29:23

A man's pride shall bring him low: but honour shall uphold the humble in spirit.

JUSTNESS

Proverbs 3:33

The curse of the Lord *is* in the house of the wicked: but he blesseth the habitation of the just.

Proverbs 4:18

But the path of the just *is* as the shining light, that shineth more and more unto the perfect day.

Proverbs 9:9

Give *instruction* to a wise *man*, and he will be yet wiser: teach a just *man*, and he will increase in learning.

Proverbs 10:6

Blessings *are* upon the head of the just: but violence covereth the mouth of the wicked.

Proverbs 10:7

The memory of the just *is* blessed: but the name of the wicked shall rot.

Proverbs 10:20

The tongue of the just *is as* choice silver: the heart of the wicked *is* little worth.

Proverbs 10:31

The mouth of the just bringeth forth wisdom: but the froward tongue shall be cut out.

Proverbs 11:9

An hypocrite with *his* mouth destroyeth his neighbour: but through knowledge shall the just be delivered.

Proverbs 12:13

The wicked is snared by the transgression of *his* lips: but the just shall come out of trouble.

Proverbs 12:21

There shall no evil happen to the just: but the wicked shall be filled with mischief.

Proverbs 16:11

A just weight and balance *are* the Lord's: all the weights of the bag *are* his work.

Proverbs 17:15

He that justifieth the wicked, and he that condemneth the just, even they both *are* abomination to the Lord.

Proverbs 17:26

Also to punish the just *is* not good, *nor* to strike princes for equity.

Proverbs 20:7

The just *man* walketh in his integrity: his children *are* blessed after him.

Proverbs 21:3

To do justice and judgment *is* more acceptable to the Lord than sacrifice.

Proverbs 21:15

It is joy to the just to do judgment: but destruction *shall be* to the workers of iniquity.

Proverbs 24:16

For a just *man* falleth seven times, and riseth up again: but the wicked shall fall into mischief.

Proverbs 28:8

He that by usury and unjust gain increaseth his substance, he shall gather it for him that will pity the poor.

Proverbs 29:10

The bloodthirsty hate the upright: but the just seek his
soul.

Proverbs 29:27

An unjust man *is* an abomination to the just: and *he
that is* upright in the way *is* abomination to the wicked.

MERCY

Proverbs 11:17

The merciful man doeth good to his own soul: but *he that is* cruel troubleth his own flesh.

Proverbs 14:21

He that despiseth his neighbour sinneth: but he that hath mercy on the poor, happy *is* he.

Proverbs 14:22

Do they not err that devise evil? but mercy and truth *shall be* to them that devise good.

Proverbs 14:31

He that oppresseth the poor reproacheth his Maker: but he that honoureth him hath mercy on the poor.

Proverbs 21:21

He that followeth after righteousness and mercy findeth life, righteousness, and honour.

RIGHTEOUSNESS

Proverbs 2:6,7

For the Lord giveth wisdom: out of his mouth *cometh* knowledge and understanding.

He layeth up sound wisdom for the righteous: *he is* a buckler to them that walk uprightly.

Proverbs 10:2

Treasures of wickedness profit nothing: but righteousness delivereth from death.

Proverbs 10:3

The Lord will not suffer the soul of the righteous to famish: but he casteth away the substance of the wicked.

Proverbs 10:11

The mouth of a righteous *man is* a well of life: but violence covereth the mouth of the wicked.

Proverbs 10:16

The labour of the righteous *tendeth* to life: the fruit of the wicked to sin.

Proverbs 10:21

The lips of the righteous feed many: but fools die for want of wisdom.

Proverbs 10:24

The fear of the wicked, it shall come upon him: but the desire of the righteous shall be granted.

Proverbs 10:25

As the whirlwind passeth, so *is* the wicked no *more:* but the righteous *is* an everlasting foundation.

Proverbs 10:28

The hope of the righteous *shall be* gladness: but the expectation of the wicked shall perish.

Proverbs 10:30

The righteous shall never be removed: but the wicked shall not inhabit the earth.

Proverbs 10:32

The lips of the righteous know what is acceptable: but the mouth of the wicked *speaketh* frowardness.

Proverbs 11:4

Riches profit not in the day of wrath: but righteousness delivereth from death.

Proverbs 11:5

The righteousness of the perfect shall direct his way: but the wicked shall fall by his own wickedness.

Proverbs 11:8

The righteous is delivered out of trouble, and the wicked cometh in his stead.

Proverbs 11:18

The wicked worketh a deceitful work: but to him that soweth righteousness *shall be* a sure reward.

Proverbs 11:19

As righteousness *tendeth* to life: so he that pursueth evil *pursueth it* to his own death.

Proverbs 11:21

Though hand *join* in hand, the wicked shall not be unpunished: but the seed of the righteous shall be delivered.

Proverbs 11:28

He that trusteth in his riches shall fall: but the righteous
shall flourish as a branch.

Proverbs 11:30

The fruit of the righteous *is* a tree of life; and he that
winneth souls *is* wise.

Proverbs 11:31

Behold, the righteous shall be recompensed in the earth:
much more the wicked and the sinner.

Proverbs 12:3

A man shall not be established by wickedness: but the
root of the righteous shall not be moved.

Proverbs 12:5

The thoughts of the righteous *are* right: *but* the counsels
of the wicked *are* deceit.

Proverbs 12:7

The wicked are overthrown, and *are* not: but the house of the righteous shall stand.

Proverbs 12:10

A righteous *man* regardeth the life of his beast: but the tender mercies of the wicked *are* cruel.

Proverbs 12:12

The wicked desireth the net of evil *men*: but the root of the righteous yieldeth *fruit*.

Proverbs 12:17

He that speaketh truth sheweth forth righteousness: but a false witness deceit.

Proverbs 12:26

The righteous *is* more excellent than his neighbour: but the way of the wicked seduceth them.

Proverbs 12:28

In the way of righteousness *is* life; and *in* the pathway *thereof there is* no death.

Proverbs 13:5

A righteous *man* hateth lying: but a wicked *man* is loathsome, and cometh to shame.

Proverbs 13:6

Righteousness keepeth *him that is* upright in the way: but wickedness overthroweth the sinner.

Proverbs 13:9

The light of the righteous rejoiceth: but the lamp of the wicked shall be put out.

Proverbs 13:21

Evil pursueth sinners: but to the righteous good shall be repayed.

Proverbs 13:25

The righteous eateth to the satisfying of his soul: but the belly of the wicked shall want.

Proverbs 14:9

Fools make a mock at sin: but among the righteous *there is* favour.

Proverbs 14:19

The evil bow before the good; and the wicked at the gates of the righteous.

Proverbs 14:32

The wicked is driven away in his wickedness: but the righteous hath hope in his death.

Proverbs 14:34

Righteousness exalteth a nation: but sin *is* a reproach to any people.

Proverbs 15:6

In the house of the righteous *is* much treasure: but in the revenues of the wicked is trouble.

Proverbs 15:9

The way of the wicked *is* an abomination unto the Lord: but he loveth him that followeth after righteousness.

Proverbs 15:19

The way of the slothful *man is* as an hedge of thorns: but the way of the righteous *is* made plain.

Proverbs 15:28

The heart of the righteous studieth to answer: but the mouth of the wicked poureth out evil things.

Proverbs 15:29

The Lord *is* far from the wicked: but he heareth the prayer of the righteous.

Proverbs 16:8

Better *is* a little with righteousness than great revenues without right.

Proverbs 16:12

It is an abomination to kings to commit wickedness: for the throne is established by righteousness.

Proverbs 18:5

It is not good to accept the person of the wicked, to overthrow the righteous in judgment.

Proverbs 18:10

The name of the Lord *is* a strong tower: the righteous runneth into it, and is safe.

Proverbs 21:12

The righteous *man* wisely considereth the house of the wicked: *but God* overthroweth the wicked for *their* wickedness.

Proverbs 21:18

The wicked *shall be* a ransom for the righteous, and the transgressor for the upright.

Proverbs 21:21

He that followeth after righteousness and mercy findeth life, righteousness, and honour.

Proverbs 21:25,26

The desire of the slothful killeth him; for his hands refuse to labour.

He coveteth greedily all the day long: but the righteous giveth and spareth not.

Proverbs 23:24

The father of the righteous shall greatly rejoice: and he that begetteth a wise *child* shall have joy of him.

Proverbs 25:26

A righteous man falling down before the wicked *is as* a troubled fountain, and a corrupt spring.

Proverbs 28:1

The wicked flee when no man pursueth: but the righteous are bold as a lion.

Proverbs 28:10

Whoso causeth the righteous to go astray in an evil way, he shall fall himself into his own pit: but the upright shall have good *things* in possession.

Proverbs 28:12

When righteous *men* do rejoice, *there is* great glory: but when the wicked rise, a man is hidden.

Proverbs 28:28

When the wicked rise, men hide themselves: but when they perish, the righteous increase.

Proverbs 29:6

In the transgression of an evil man *there is* a snare: but the righteous doth sing and rejoice.

Proverbs 29:7

The righteous considereth the cause of the poor: *but* the wicked regardeth not to know *it*.

Proverbs 29:16

When the wicked are multiplied, transgression increaseth: but the righteous shall see their fall.

STRENGTH

Proverbs 10:29

The way of the Lord *is* strength to the upright: but destruction *shall be* to the workers of iniquity.

Proverbs 11:16

A gracious woman retaineth honour: and strong *men* retain riches.

Proverbs 20:29

The glory of young men *is* their strength: and the beauty of old men *is* the gray head.

Proverbs 24:5

A wise man *is* strong; yea, a man of knowledge increaseth strength.

Proverbs 24:10

If thou faint in the day of adversity, thy strength *is* small.

UPRIGHTNESS

Proverbs 2:7

He layeth up sound wisdom for the righteous: *he is* a buckler to them that walk uprightly.

Proverbs 2:21,22

For the upright shall dwell in the land, and the perfect shall remain in it.

But the wicked shall be cut off from the earth, and the transgressors shall be rooted out of it.

Proverbs 10:9

He that walketh uprightly walketh surely: but he that perverteth his ways shall be known.

Proverbs 10:29

The way of the Lord *is* strength to the upright: but destruction *shall be* to the workers of iniquity.

Proverbs 11:3

The integrity of the upright shall guide them: but the perverseness of transgressors shall destroy them.

Proverbs 11:6

The righteousness of the upright shall deliver them: but transgressors shall be taken in *their own* naughtiness.

Proverbs 11:11

By the blessing of the upright the city is exalted: but it is overthrown by the mouth of the wicked.

Proverbs 11:20

They that are of a froward heart *are* abomination to the Lord: but *such as are* upright in *their* way *are* his delight.

Proverbs 12:6

The words of the wicked *are* to lie in wait for blood: but the mouth of the upright shall deliver them.

Proverbs 13:6

Righteousness keepeth *him that is* upright in the way: but wickedness overthroweth the sinner.

Proverbs 14:2

He that walketh in his uprightness feareth the Lord: but *he that is* perverse in his ways despiseth him.

Proverbs 14:11

The house of the wicked shall be overthrown: but the tabernacle of the upright shall flourish.

Proverbs 15:8

The sacrifice of the wicked *is* an abomination to the Lord: but the prayer of the upright *is* his delight.

Proverbs 15:21

Folly *is* joy to *him that is* destitute of wisdom: but a man of understanding walketh uprightly.

Proverbs 16:17

The highway of the upright *is* to depart from evil: he that keepeth his way preserveth his soul.

Proverbs 21:18

The wicked *shall be* a ransom for the righteous, and the transgressor for the upright.

Proverbs 21:29

A wicked man hardeneth his face: but *as for* the upright, he directeth his way.

Proverbs 28:6

Better *is* the poor that walketh in his uprightness, than *he that is* perverse *in his* ways, though he *be* rich.

Proverbs 28:10

Whoso causeth the righteous to go astray in an evil way, he shall fall himself into his own pit: but the upright shall have good *things* in possession.

Proverbs 28:18

Whoso walketh uprightly shall be saved: but *he that is* perverse *in his* ways shall fall at once.

Proverbs 29:10

The bloodthirsty hate the upright: but the just seek his soul.

Proverbs 29:27

An unjust man *is* an abomination to the just: and *he that is* upright in the way *is* abomination to the wicked.

PART EIGHT

Prosperity

GIVING

Proverbs 3:9,10

Honour the Lord with thy substance, and with the first-fruits of all thine increase:

So shall thy barns be filled with plenty, and thy presses shall burst out with new wine.

Proverbs 3:27,28

Withhold not good from them to whom it is due, when it is in the power of thine hand to do *it*.

Say not unto thy neighbour, Go, and come again, and to morrow I will give; when thou hast it by thee.

Proverbs 11:24

There is that scattereth, and yet increaseth; and *there is* that withholdeth more than is meet, but *it tendeth* to poverty.

Proverbs 11:25

The liberal soul shall be made fat: and he that watereth shall be watered also himself.

Proverbs 19:6

Many will entreat the favour of the prince: and every man *is* a friend to him that giveth gifts.

Proverbs 19:17

He that hath pity upon the poor lendeth unto the Lord; and that which he hath given will he pay him again.

Proverbs 22:9

He that hath a bountiful eye shall be blessed; for he giveth of his bread to the poor.

Proverbs 28:27

He that giveth unto the poor shall not lack: but he that hideth his eyes shall have many a curse.

LAZINESS

Proverbs 6:6-8

Go to the ant, thou sluggard; consider her ways, and be wise:

Which having no guide, overseer, or ruler,

Provideth her meal in the summer, *and* gathereth her food in the harvest.

Proverbs 6:9-11

How long wilt thou sleep, O sluggard? when wilt thou arise out of thy sleep?

Yet a little sleep, a little slumber, a little folding of the hands to sleep:

So shall thy poverty come as one that travelleth, and thy want as an armed man.

Proverbs 10:5

He that gathereth in summer *is* a wise son: *but* he that sleepeth in harvest *is* a son that causeth shame.

Proverbs 10:26

As vinegar to the teeth, and as smoke to the eyes, so *is* the sluggard to them that send him.

Proverbs 12:24

The hand of the diligent shall bear rule: but the slothful shall be under tribute.

Proverbs 12:27

The slothful *man* roasteth not that which he took in hunting: but the substance of a diligent man *is* precious.

Proverbs 13:4

The soul of the sluggard desireth, and *hath* nothing: but the soul of the diligent shall be made fat.

Proverbs 15:19

The way of the slothful *man is* as an hedge of thorns: but the way of the righteous *is* made plain.

Proverbs 18:9

He also that is slothful in his work is brother to him that is a great waster.

Proverbs 19:15

Slothfulness casteth into a deep sleep; and an idle soul shall suffer hunger.

Proverbs 19:24

A slothful *man* hideth his hand in *his* bosom, and will not so much as bring it to him mouth again.

Proverbs 20:4

The sluggard will not plow by reason of the cold; *therefore* shall he beg in harvest, and *have* nothing.

Proverbs 21:25,26

The desire of the slothful killeth him; for his hands refuse to labour.

He coveteth greedily all the day long: but the righteous giveth and spareth not.

Proverbs 24:30-34

I went by the field of the slothful, and by the vineyard of the man void of understanding;

And, lo, it was all grown over with thorns, *and* nettles had covered the face thereof, and the stone wall thereof was broken down.

Then I saw, *and* considered *it* well: I looked upon *it*, *and* received instruction.

Yet a little sleep, a little slumber, a little folding of the hands to sleep:

So shall thy poverty come *as* one that travelleth; and thy want as an armed man.

Proverbs 26:13,14

The slothful *man* saith, *There is* a lion in the way; a lion *is* in the streets.

As the door turneth upon his hinges, so *doth* the slothful upon his bed.

Proverbs 26:15

The slothful hideth his hand in *his* bosom; it grieveth him to bring it again to his mouth.

Proverbs 26:16

The sluggard *is* wiser in his own conceit than seven men that can render a reason.

PROSPERITY

Proverbs 3:13-15

Happy *is* the man *that* findeth wisdom, and the man *that* getteth understanding.

For the merchandise of it *is* better than the merchandise of silver, and the gain thereof than fine gold.

She *is* more precious than rubies: and all the things thou canst desire are not to be compared unto her.

Proverbs 8:14,18-21

Counsel *is* mine, and sound wisdom: I *am* understanding; I have strength.

Riches and honour *are* with me; *yea,* durable riches and righteousness.

My fruit *is* better than gold, yea, than fine gold; and my revenue than choice silver.

I lead in the way of righteousness, in the midst of the paths of judgment:

That I may cause those that love me to inherit substance; and I will fill their treasures.

Proverbs 10:2

Treasures of wickedness profit nothing: but righteousness delivereth from death.

Proverbs 10:3

The Lord will not suffer the soul of the righteous to famish: but he casteth away the substance of the wicked.

Proverbs 10:22

The blessing of the Lord, it maketh rich, and he addeth no sorrow with it.

Proverbs 10:24

The fear of the wicked, it shall come upon him: but the desire of the righteous shall be granted.

Proverbs 11:4

Riches profit not in the day of wrath: but righteousness delivereth from death.

Proverbs 11:28

He that trusteth in his riches shall fall: but the righteous shall flourish as a branch.

Proverbs 13:7

There is that maketh himself rich, yet *hath* nothing: *there is* that maketh himself poor, yet *hath* great riches.

Proverbs 13:11

Wealth *gotten* by vanity shall be diminished: but he that gathereth by labour shall increase.

Proverbs 15:6

In the house of the righteous *is* much treasure: but in the revenues of the wicked is trouble.

Proverbs 15:16

Better *is* little with the fear of the Lord than great treasure and trouble therewith.

Proverbs 15:17

Better *is* a dinner of herbs where love is, than a stalled ox and hatred therewith.

Proverbs 15:27

He that is greedy of gain troubleth his own house; but he that hateth gifts shall live.

Proverbs 16:8

Better *is* a little with righteousness than great revenues without right.

Proverbs 17:1

Better *is* a dry morsel, and quietness therewith, than an house full of sacrifices *with* strife.

Proverbs 18:16

A man's gift maketh room for him, and bringeth him before great men.

Proverbs 20:21

An inheritance *may be* gotten hastily at the beginning; but the end thereof shall not be blessed.

Proverbs 21:6

The getting of treasures by a lying tongue *is* a vanity tossed to and fro of them that seek death.

Proverbs 21:17

He that loveth pleasure *shall be* a poor man: he that loveth wine and oil shall not be rich.

Proverbs 22:1

A *good* name *is* rather to be chosen than great riches, *and* loving favour rather than silver and gold.

Proverbs 22:4

By humility *and* the fear of the Lord *are* riches, and honour, and life.

Proverbs 22:16

He that oppresseth the poor to increase his *riches, and* he that giveth to the rich, *shall* surely *come* to want.

Proverbs 23:4,5

Labour not to be rich: cease from thine own wisdom.

Wilt thou set thine eyes upon that which is not? for *riches* certainly make themselves wings; they fly away as an eagle toward heaven.

Proverbs 24:3,4

Through wisdom is an house builded; and by understanding it is established:

And by knowledge shall the chambers be filled with all precious and pleasant riches.

Proverbs 28:6

Better *is* the poor that walketh in his uprightness, than *he that is* perverse *in his* ways, though he *be* rich.

Proverbs 28:8

He that by usury and unjust gain increaseth his substance, he shall gather it for him that will pity the poor.

Proverbs 28:10

Whoso causeth the righteous to go astray in an evil way, he shall fall himself into his own pit: but the upright shall have good *things* in possession.

Proverbs 28:11

The rich man *is* wise in his own conceit; but the poor that hath understanding searcheth him out.

Proverbs 28:13

He that covereth his sins shall not prosper: but whoso confesseth and forsaketh *them* shall have mercy.

Proverbs 28:19

He that tilleth his land shall have plenty of bread: but he that followeth after vain *persons* shall have poverty enough.

Proverbs 28:20

A faithful man shall abound with blessings: but he that maketh haste to be rich shall not be innocent.

Proverbs 28:22

He that hasteth to be rich *hath* an evil eye, and considereth not that poverty shall come upon him.

Proverbs 30:8,9

Remove far from me vanity and lies: give me neither poverty nor riches; feed me with food convenient for me:

Lest I be full, and deny *thee*, and say, Who *is* the Lord? or lest I be poor, and steal, and take the name of my God *in vain.*

STEWARDSHIP

Proverbs 10:4

He becometh poor that dealeth *with* a slack hand: but the hand of the diligent maketh rich.

Proverbs 12:11

He that tilleth his land shall be satisfied with bread: but he that followeth vain *persons is* void of understanding.

Proverbs 12:27

The slothful *man* roasteth not that which he took in hunting: but the substance of a diligent man *is* precious.

Proverbs 27:23,27

Be thou diligent to know the state of thy flocks, *and* look well to thy herds.

And *thou shalt have* goats' milk enough for thy food, for the food of thy household, and *for* the maintenance for thy maidens.

SURETY

Proverbs 6:1-5

My son, if thou be surety for thy friend, *if* thou hast stricken thy hand with a stranger,

Thou art snared with the words of thy mouth, thou art taken with the words of thy mouth.

Do this now, my son, and deliver thyself, when thou art come into the hand of thy friend; go, humble thyself, and make sure thy friend.

Give not sleep to thine eyes, nor slumber to thine eyelids.

Deliver thyself as a roe from the hand *of the hunter*, and as a bird from the hand of the fowler.

Proverbs 11:15

He that is surety for a stranger shall smart *for it*: and he that hateth suretiship is sure.

Proverbs 17:18

A man void of understanding striketh hands, *and* becometh surety in the presence of his friend.

Proverbs 22:26,27

Be not thou *one* of them that strike hands, *or* of them that are sureties for debts.

If thou hast nothing to pay, why should he take away thy bed from under thee?

WORK

Proverbs 6:6-8

Go to the ant, thou sluggard; consider her ways, and be wise:

Which having no guide, overseer, or ruler,

Provideth her meal in the summer, *and* gathereth her food in the harvest.

Proverbs 10:4

He becometh poor that dealeth *with* a slack hand: but the hand of the diligent maketh rich.

Proverbs 10:5

He that gathereth in summer *is* a wise son: *but* he that sleepeth in harvest *is* a son that causeth shame.

Proverbs 10:16

The labour of the righteous *tendeth* to life: the fruit of the wicked to sin.

Proverbs 12:11

He that tilleth his land shall be satisfied with bread: but he that followeth vain *persons is* void of understanding.

Proverbs 12:14

A man shall be satisfied with good by the fruit of *his* mouth: and the recompense of a man's hands shall be rendered unto him.

Proverbs 12:24

The hand of the diligent shall bear rule: but the slothful shall be under tribute.

Proverbs 12:27

The slothful *man* roasteth not that which he took in hunting: but the substance of a diligent man *is* precious.

Proverbs 13:4

The soul of the sluggard desireth, and *hath* nothing: but the soul of the diligent shall be made fat.

Proverbs 13:11

Wealth *gotten* by vanity shall be diminished: but he that gathereth by labour shall increase.

Proverbs 14:23

In all labour there is profit: but the talk of the lips *tendeth* only to penury.

Proverbs 16:3

Commit thy works unto the Lord, and thy thoughts shall be established.

Proverbs 16:26

He that laboureth laboureth for himself; for his mouth craveth it of him.

Proverbs 18:9

He also that is slothful in his work is brother to him that is a great waster.

Proverbs 20:11

Even a child is known by his doings, whether his work *be* pure, and whether *it be* right.

Proverbs 22:29

Seest thou a man diligent in his business? he shall stand before kings; he shall not stand before mean *men.*

Proverbs 24:27

Prepare thy work without, and make it fit for thyself in the field; and afterwards build thine house.

Proverbs 27:18

Whoso keepeth the fig tree shall eat the fruit thereof: so he that waiteth on his master shall be honoured.

Proverbs 27:23,27

Be thou diligent to know the state of thy flocks, *and* look well to thy herds.

And *thou shalt have* goats' milk enough for thy food, for the food of thy household, and *for* the maintenance for thy maidens.

Proverbs 28:19

He that tilleth his land shall have plenty of bread: but he that followeth after vain *persons* shall have poverty enough.